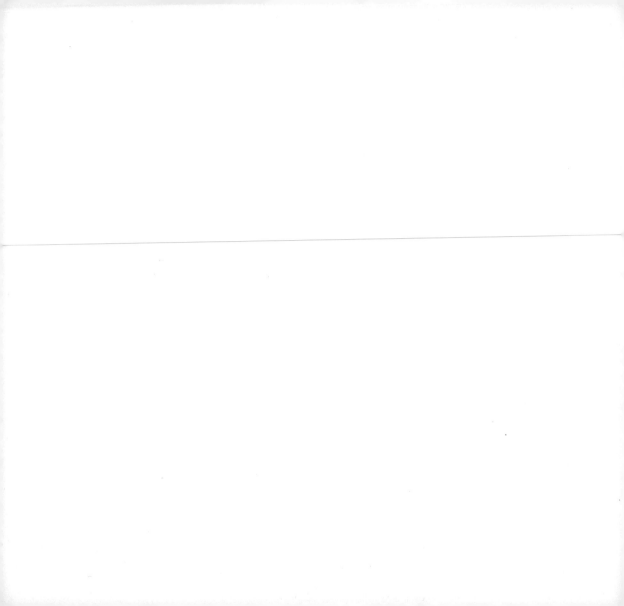

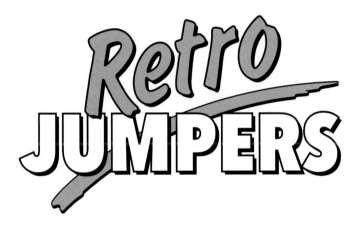

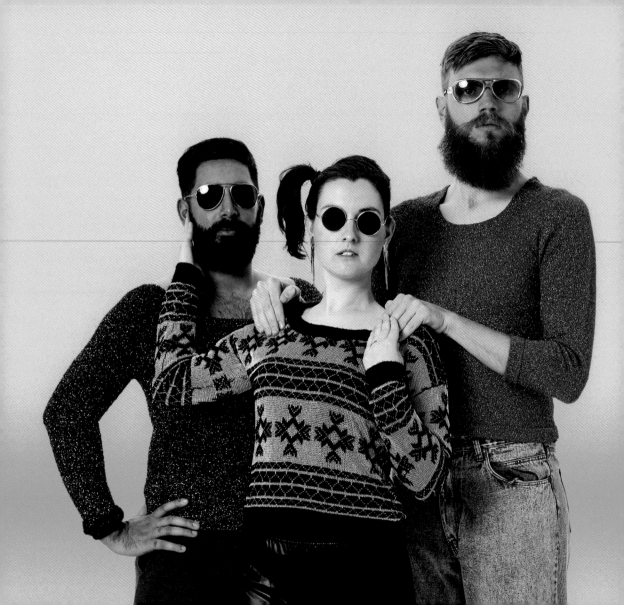

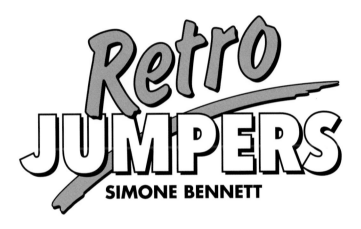

SIMONE BENNETT

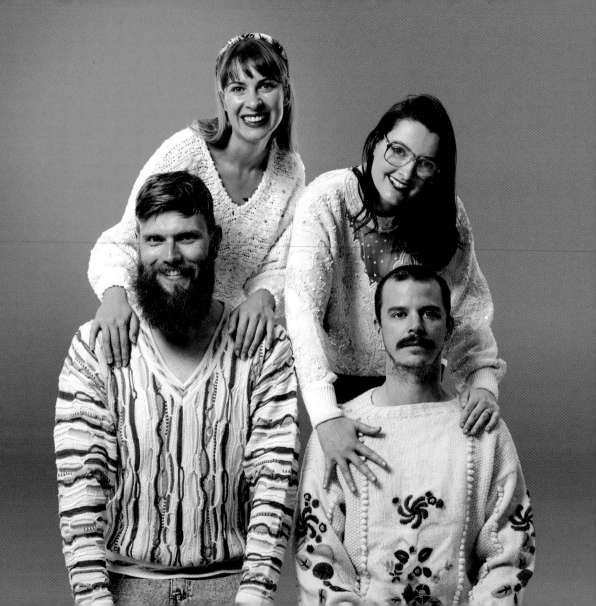

Let's go retro!

Yes! Hello and welcome to this very important vintage lookbook for sassy people.

As a retro fashionista, I fossick and scrounge for all sorts of vintage items – but my passion is sweaters. There are many names for these long-sleeved garments that bring us so much joy: jumpers, pullovers, woolly body-huggers. If there were no sweaters, then where would we be? Cold, topless and depressed, with no way to express our love of retro style.

This book showcases a collection of ensembles inspired by the 1960s, '70s, '80s and '90s when frankly, everything was better. Fashion was fun, music was great and women knew their place. There are outfits for any occasion: dancing, hosting a dinner party, using computers, swimming – or, you know, just being casual.

People often ask me 'Simone, how did you get so good at clothes?' and I just laugh at them. Fashion sense is something you're born with. Knowing which sassy knit goes with what fancy hat is something that comes naturally to me. But through diligent study, you can probably learn. The knowledge you gain from this book will not only help you look interesting and attractive – like me – but will help you be a better human and achieve your dreams. You'll instantly see the results in all areas of your life, from the boardroom to the bedroom.

Fashionably yours,

Simone Bennett

Simone Bennett
Author and sweater collector

Collect your own

Finding the good stuff takes more than luck. You must swoop in like a hawk and have an eagle eye to sort the treasure from the trash. Let me take you under my shoulder-padded wing.

THRIFT STORES

Thrift stores are magical places. Befriend the staff and find out what day new shipments typically arrive. Inner-city stores are picked over by the hipsters, so travel out of town to find the most unique items. Avoid long lines for the change room by wearing a skin-tight body stocking, allowing you to try on clothes over the top (this will also help you feel sexy while you shop, which is important).

OLD PEOPLE

The elderly are selfishly hoarding all the best sweaters and you need to be cunning to gain access. When your grandma falls asleep watching her game show, go shopping in her wardrobe and attic. If your grandparents are no longer with us, simply befriend the old lady next door and make her endless cups of tea. She'll definitely leave you suitcases full of vintage clothing in her will.

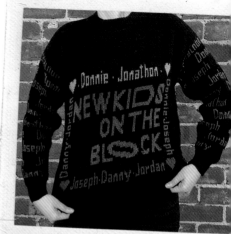

Best boy band ever!

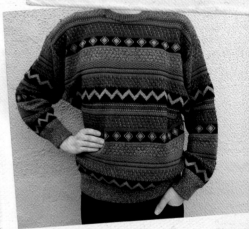

'60s style Coogi madness

GARAGE SALES

Get there EARLY. I'm talking 4am. Bring a deck chair and just wait on the sidewalk. Then you'll be ready to start rifling through boxes as the sellers set up. Don't be put off by dirty looks and snide remarks. Keep your eye on the prize.

DUMPSTERS

I once found a vintage Coogi in a dumpster. But please wear gloves! Needlestick injuries are real.

LOVERS

If you see someone with a particularly wonderful sweater, seduce them. Afterwards, when they are sleeping, you can pick it up off the floor and slip away into the night.

THE INTERNET

I own a personal computer, but my dial-up connection does not allow me to download pictures. My nephew tells me that you can surf into a website and purchase clothing. Give it a try!

KNIT YOUR OWN

There are plenty of amazing vintage sweater patterns around. Once you've conquered the formidable learning curve, you will find knitting rewarding and enjoyable. Personally, I hate it.

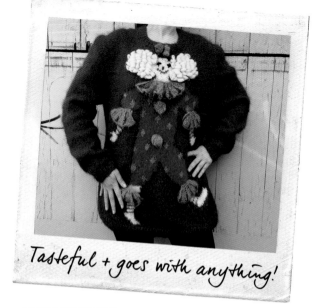

Tasteful + goes with anything!

MORE HOT TIPS

- Remember to check the fabric for stains, cigarette burns and lice.

- Buddy Up! An honest friend can tell you if you look awful in a good way, or genuinely awful (there is a difference).

- Coffee and energy drinks will help keep you focused and alert as you shop. Also bring a bunch of bananas.

- Moths are the butterfly's uglier, hungrier cousin, so use mothballs in your closet. Cover the smell of mothballs with hanging sacks of potpourri. Cover the smell of potpourri with incense.

It's your moment

BOOM. TIME TO SHINE.

If you were going for the 'flamboyant figure skater about to win gold in the 1984 Sarajevo Olympics' look, then this sweater would be a fabulous choice. Exquisite hand-stitched embroidery and detailed beading all come together in a symphony of cream.

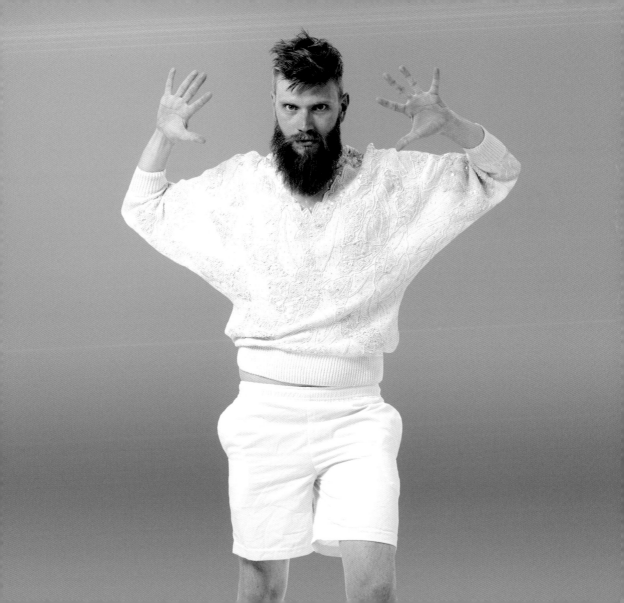

Lady in red

THE LARGEST KNIT LEGALLY AVAILABLE

Lose yourself in an oppressively large knit made in Soviet
Russia. Their sweaters were thick and fleecy and left citizens
feeling uncomfortably warm. The top-heavy shape of this
design cuts a flattering silhouette and slims the legs.
Don't forget to confuse this winter look with a sunhat.

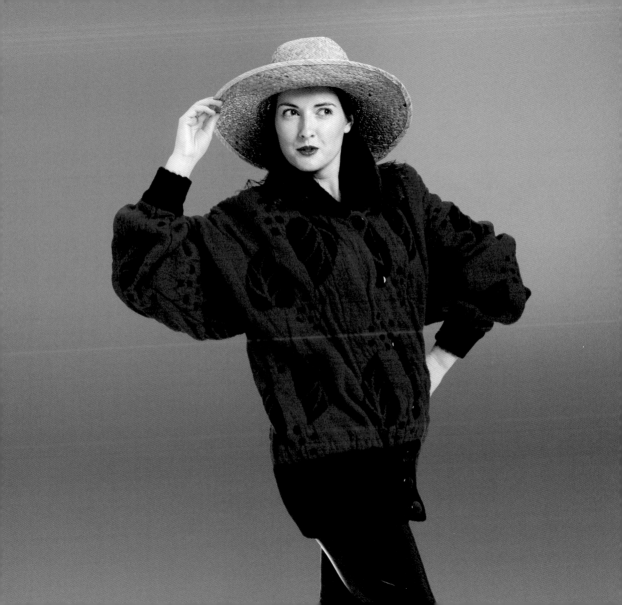

The leader is great!

FASHION THAT'S GAINING A CULT FOLLOWING

Say goodbye to your family and hello to a standard-issue crochet smock. This one features a hexagon pattern representing the six pillars of Comet's Gate – love, fellowship, music, oxygen, polygamy and fruit. The looser weave in the lower half of this garment allows important energy to reach your inner thighs.

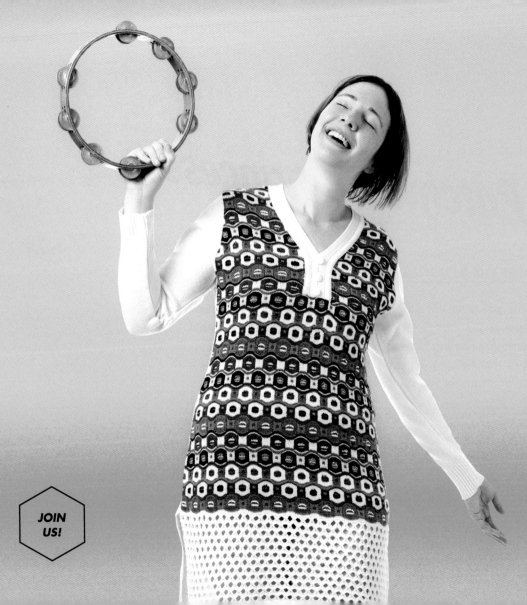

JOIN
US!

Patchwork princess

GET THE DESIGNER LOOK FOR LESS

Are you poor but desperately seeking the social validation that comes from wearing the latest couture? Wear offcuts! Just visit the big fashion labels' warehouses and sweep up the bits that fall on the factory floor. Then indiscriminately sew them together to form new and confusing designs.

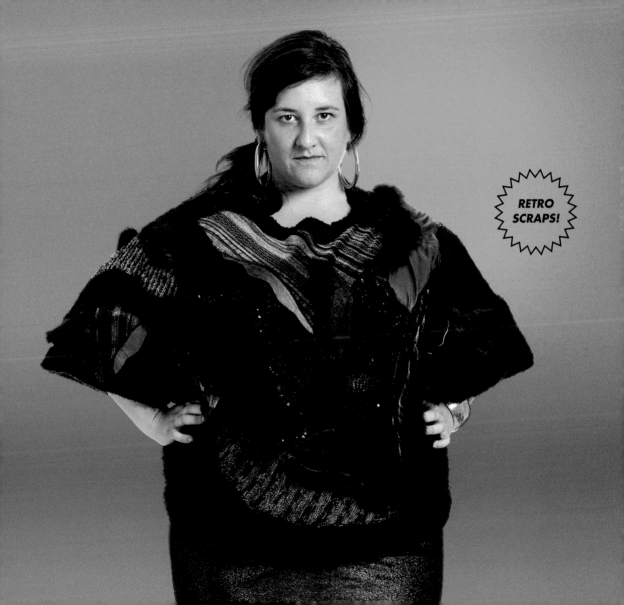

RETRO
SCRAPS!

Sick tricks!

TOTALLY GNARLY OLD SCHOOL GEAR

Skate the streets like a radical freestyle champ in a classic crew neck with striped front and detailed, patterned sleeves. You'll be working up a sweat in the California heat, so add shorts and a sweatband for a far-out look that's outta sight. Say no to drugs!

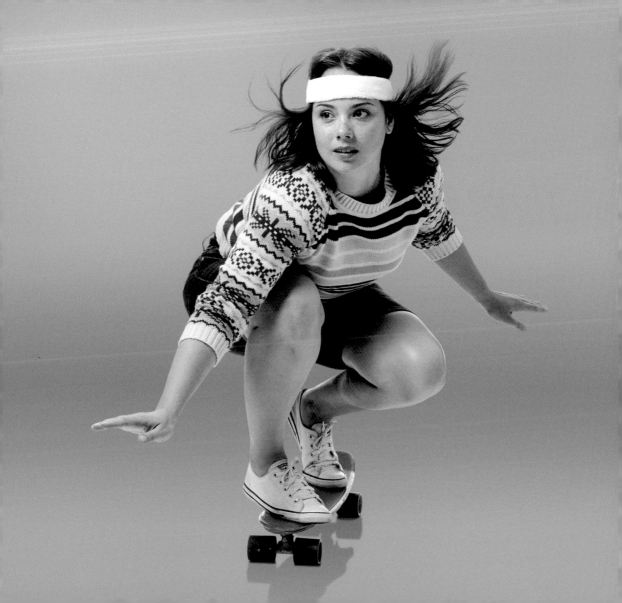

Three's company

TIGHT-KNIT FRIENDS FOREVER

Take your close friendship one step further by wearing matching sweaters! These charming knits are designed to be worn by three consenting adults and feature a quaint country scene with a little house on the prairie.

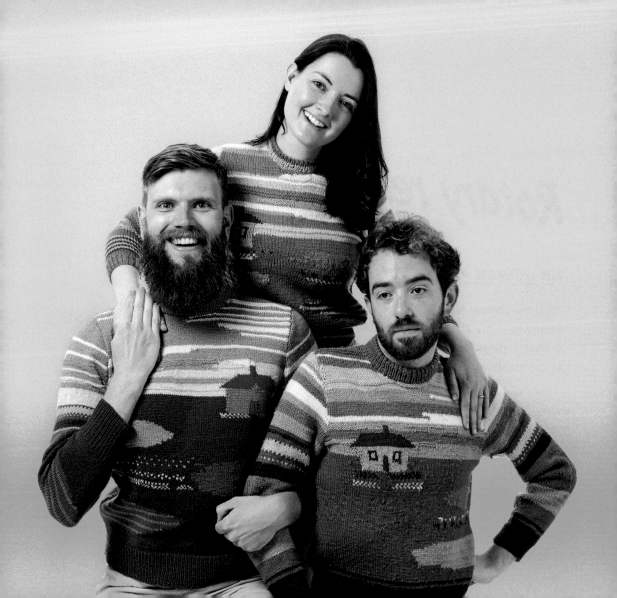

Rotary rebels

THE ULTIMATE RETRO ACCESSORY

Hold the phone! Now talk into it. Vintage fashionistas everywhere are abandoning their smartphones and going analog. Extension cords are available, so you can travel as far as the mailbox. Just ask the operator for more information.

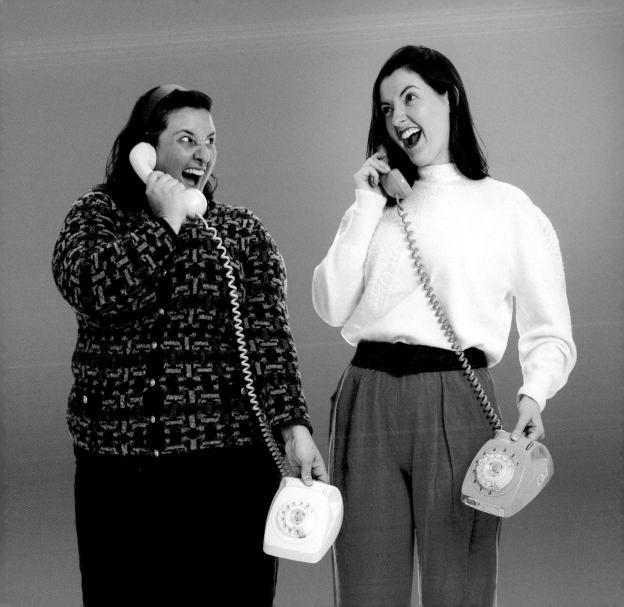

New softwear

LOOKING COOL AT COMPUTER CAMP

Defrag your wardrobe and take CTRL of your look. Hack into the mainframe wearing a geometric knit with high-resolution graphics. You and your floppy disc have never looked so good.

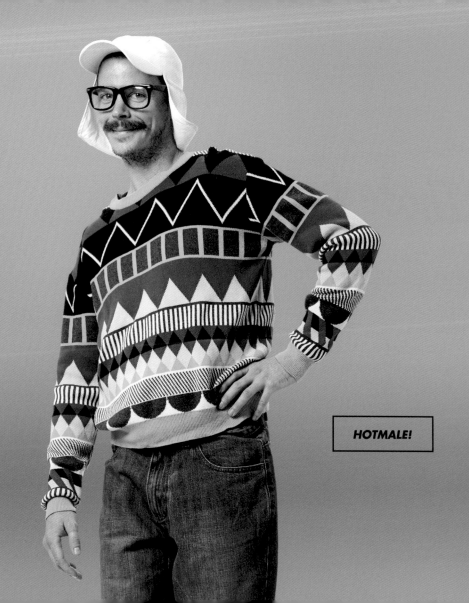

HOTMALE!

Those bows!

GIVE HIM THE GIFT OF YOU

As Coco Chanel famously quipped: *You can never have too many bows.* How right she was. This shapely sweater dress boasts a total of five bows. If you were feeling daring, you could sew on more bows. Just cover the whole thing in bows. It will be amazing.

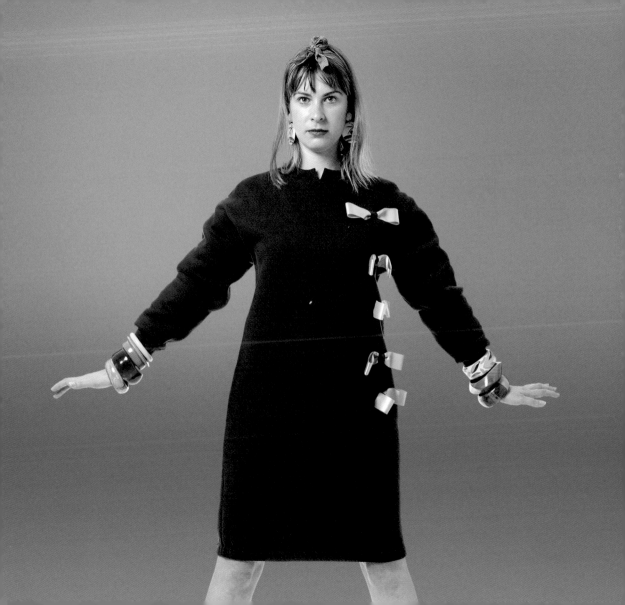

Anyone for tennis?

FASHION THAT'LL CAUSE A RACKET

When you hit the court, you'll have an advantage sporting a sweatshirt. This one features Fonzie from *Happy Days*. Game, set and matched here with a sweatband and classic Wimbledon shorts. Winning is ace. And when you lose? Hey, love hurts.

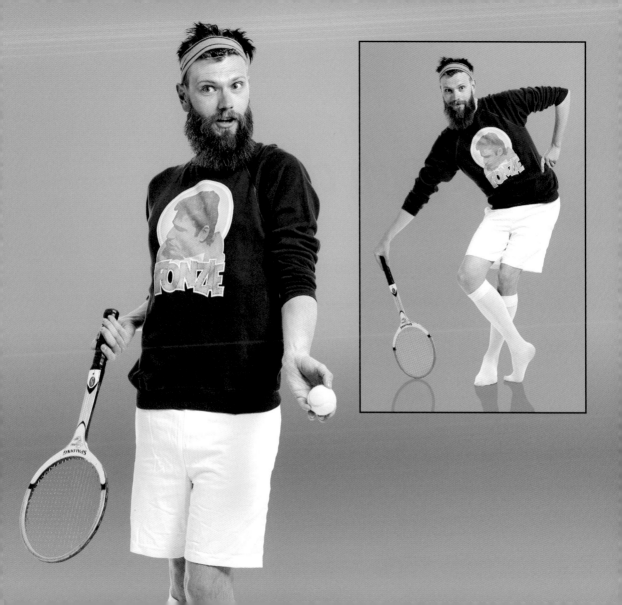

White trash chic

TWO TRAILER PARK GIRLS GO 'ROUND THE OUTSIDE

When you're invited to defend your actions on a daytime talk show, what you gonna wear? Same damn thing you wear every day! A bright as *beep* acrylic top with flowers and *beep* on it and some cut-off shorts. If that *beep* just paid his child support you wouldn't have burned down his trailer!

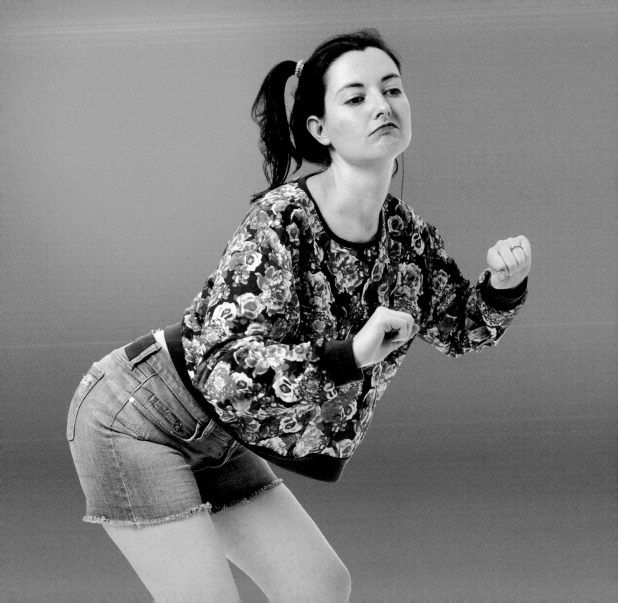

Touching moments

WINTER IS COMING. TURN UP THE HEAT.

Open fires, mulled wine and long nights trapped in the cabin –
winter is a wonderful time of year. Cuddle up and enjoy the
feeling of thick, warm fleece. This piece is warm enough for
two and features interlocking shapes and fresh, icy sparkles.

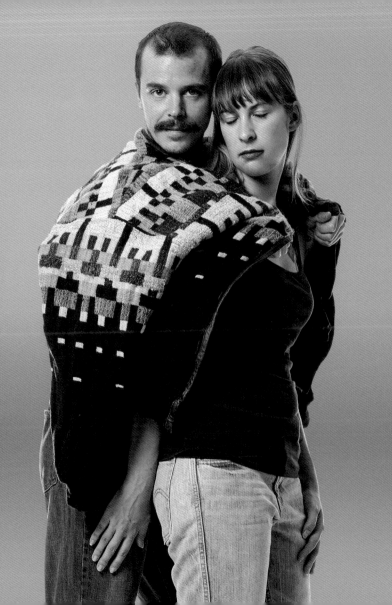

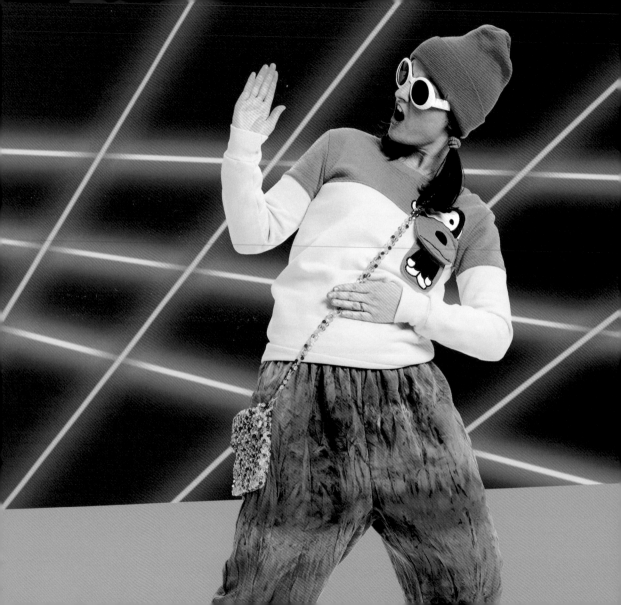

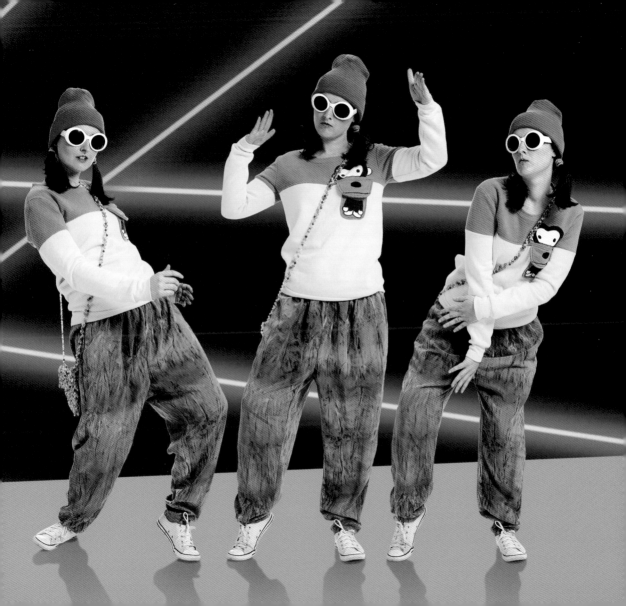

Sweet sensation

A PUBLIC SERVICE ANNOUNCEMENT

Some avant-garde sweater enthusiasts are choosing to go 'bareback'. Woah, hold your horses – this just means not wearing a t-shirt underneath. Be warned: course vintage wool can be abrasive and result in a rash. Skin irritations can be treated with a soothing gel. Ask your doctor.

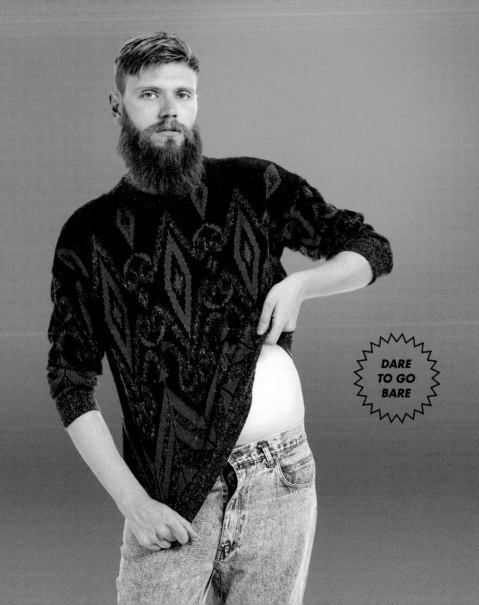

DARE
TO GO
BARE

Mellow yellow

FORM-FITTING FASHION FIT FOR FELLOWS

This yellow turtleneck is designed to flatter the male physique. Trapezoid panelling broadens the shoulders and reduces the waist, leaving you looking like a sculpted, manly banana. Mmm! Very a-peeling indeed!

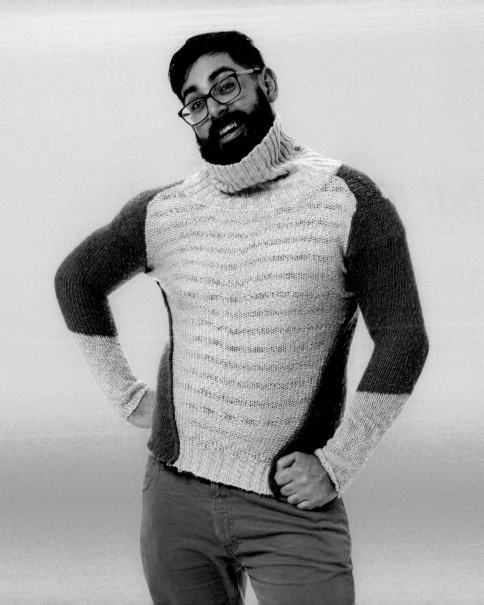

That magic touch

HAVE YOU TOUCHED SOMETHING SOFT TODAY?

You'd be pleasantly startled by the softness of these woolly warmers. Imagine a tiny rabbit quietly sleeping on a bed of marshmallows, with Enya playing in the background. That's not even getting close to how soft these sweaters are.

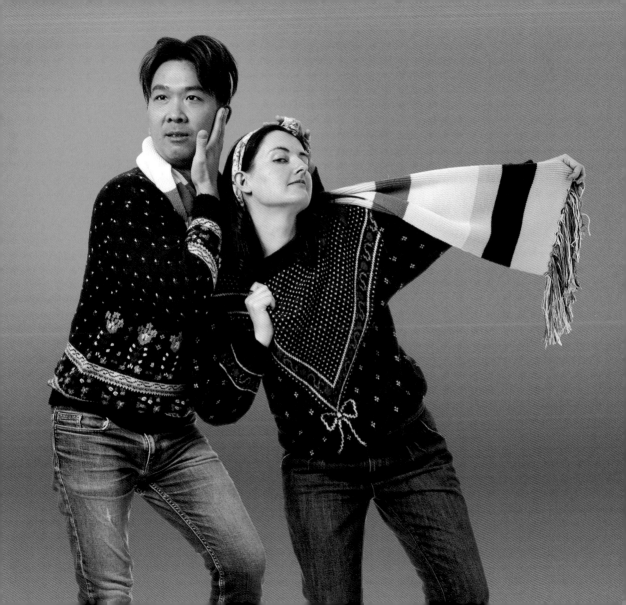

Junior fit

FEEL YOUNG AGAIN IN A GRANDMA KNIT

If you want to relive the magic of wearing a hand-knitted item lovingly made for you by an elderly relative, then why not wear an old cardigan that was clearly intended for a child? This one-off piece is nonsensical and made from the itchiest wool you can imagine. Thanks, someone's grandma!

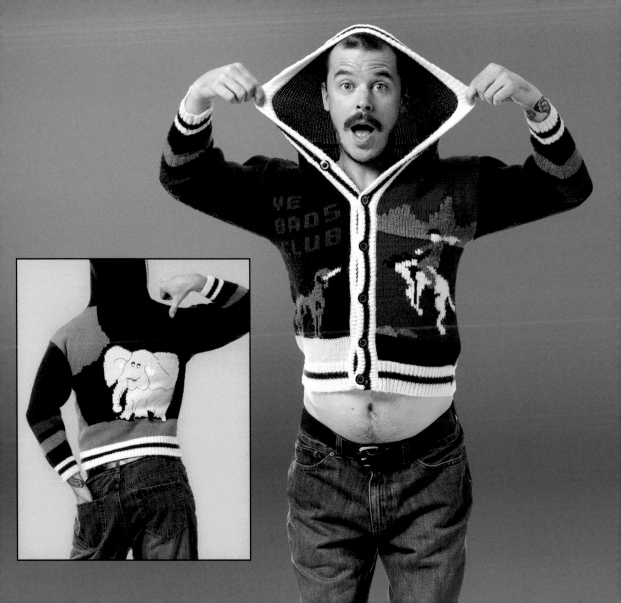

She's super!

FASHION FOR BUSY MOTHERS ON THE GO

At soccer games, you'll find her cheering and handing out oranges at half-time. At home, she's burning the meatloaf and locking herself in the bathroom with a box of wine. What a woman! She does it all in this pretty and versatile turtleneck with floral yoke.

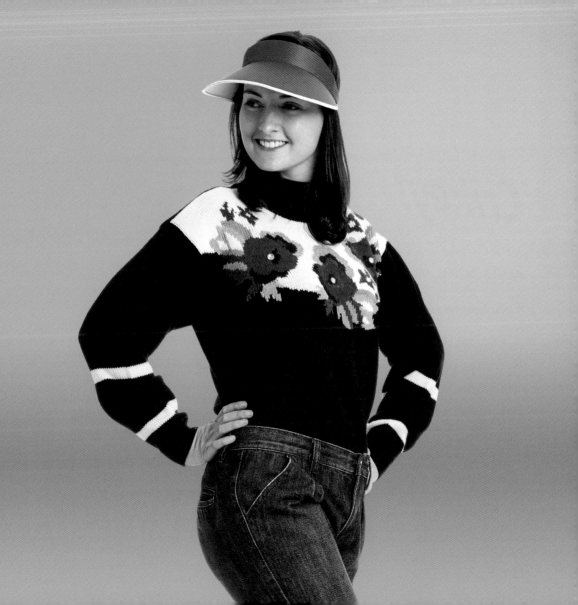

Crikey!

KNITS IN THE MIDDLE OF NOWHERE

If you ever find yourself abandoned and alone in the Australian outback, a sweater like this could help you navigate your way back to Sydney. Go past Uluṟu, head towards the Melbourne tram, then take a right. Don't stop in Wolf Creek. Good luck, mate!

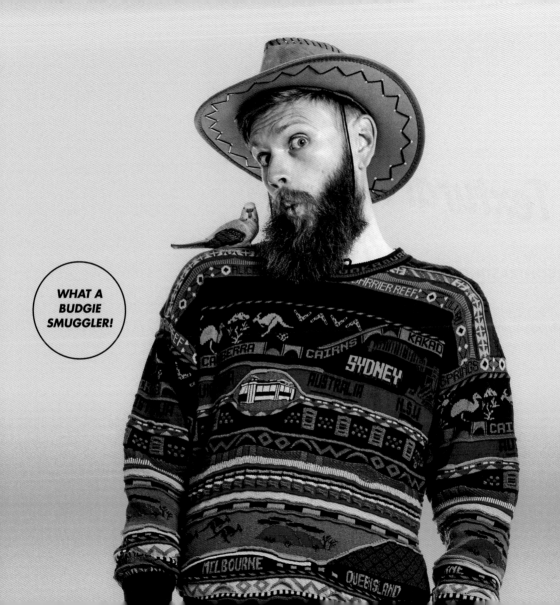

Textural healing

CONTRASTING TEXTURES MAKE THIS LOOK POP!

You could go from the library to da club in this sweet cherry top made from oh-so-tactile 'touch me' velvet. Pair a cheeky piece like this one with the right bottoms and boom! Baby got back.

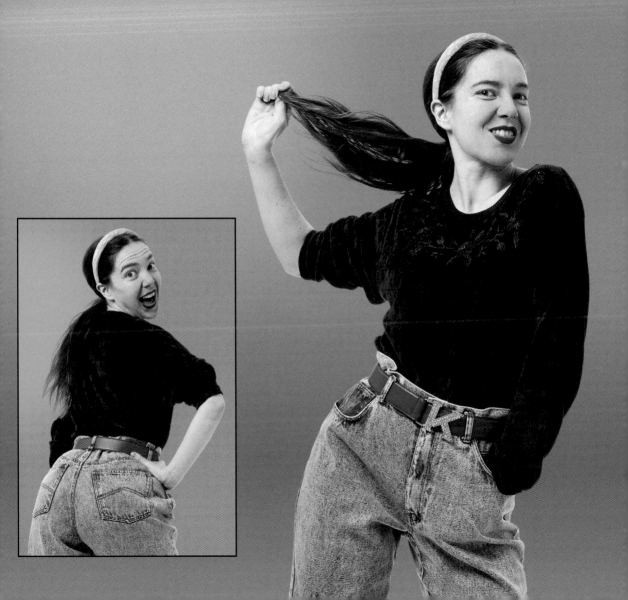

Go sports team!

KICK THE THING AND WIN THE POINTS

These pure wool jerseys are the perfect attire in which to observe an exciting game of sport. Look the part while you shout loudly and show your appreciation or disapproval for the man with the ball.

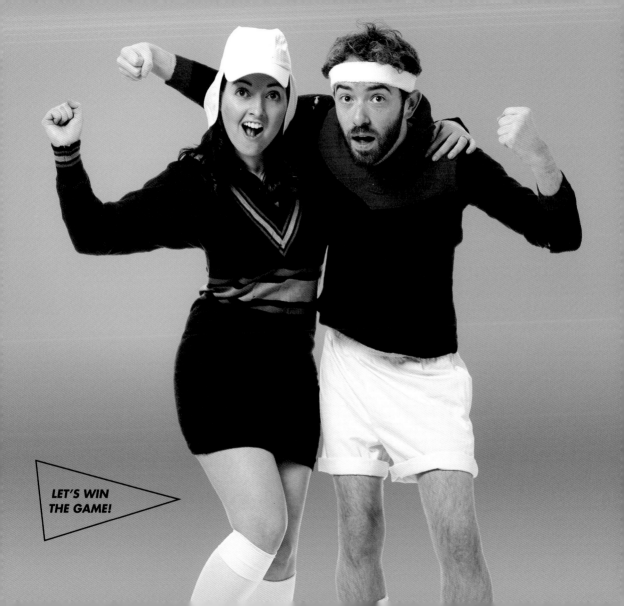

LET'S WIN
THE GAME!

Ugh, as if!

FEELING CLUELESS?

Has your wardrobe got you totally buggin'? You don't want anyone thinking you're a fashion victim or ensemble-y challenged. That's way harsh. You should totally make over your look with a Malibu pink sweater with sparkly hexagon shapes and love hearts.

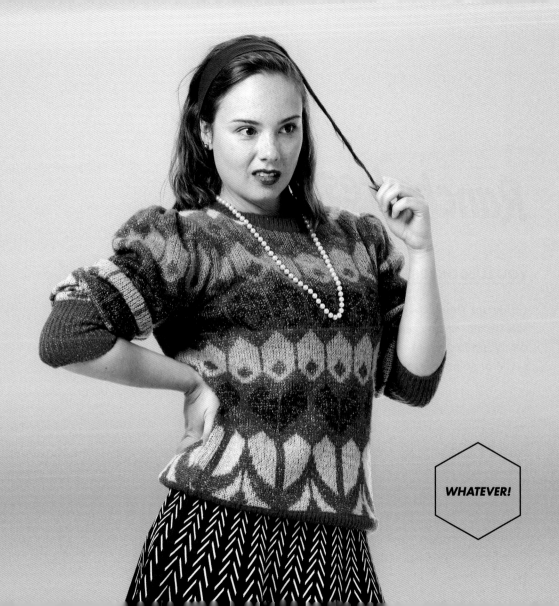

WHATEVER!

Ranch dressing

YOU'LL LOOK RIGHT AT HOME ON THE RANGE

Giddy up! There's been a stampede on vintage horse-hair sweaters in recent years – they sell like sarsaparilla on a hot day. Warm and hard-wearing, they're perfect rounding up cattle or spinning a yarn around the campfire.

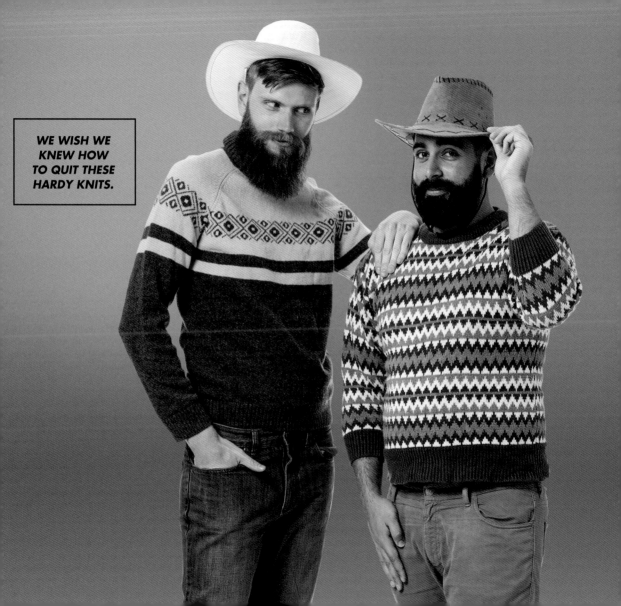

WE WISH WE KNEW HOW TO QUIT THESE HARDY KNITS.

Party on the patio

ONE SHRIMP SHORT OF A COCKTAIL

Be the hostess with the mostess in a spill-resistant knitted coat with silver sparkles. Greet your guests, make witty banter and get that salmon-and-mayonnaise gelatin log into the oven. Mmm, smells divine. A couple of valium-vodka martinis later and it's daylight. Another successful soirée, thanks to your magic hostess coat!

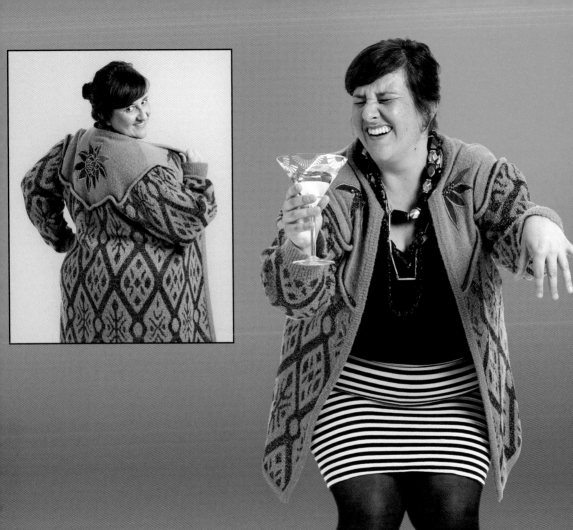

A helping hand

SHARE YOUR LIFE WITH A PUPPET FRIEND

Do you suffer from anxiety? Try sewing a 'companion sock'
into the sleeve of your sweater. You'll finally have the confidence
to speak your mind – through a puppet! Let Mrs Sock tell Shelly
at work to stop breathing loudly, or ask that sexy bartender out
on a date. Live your best life!

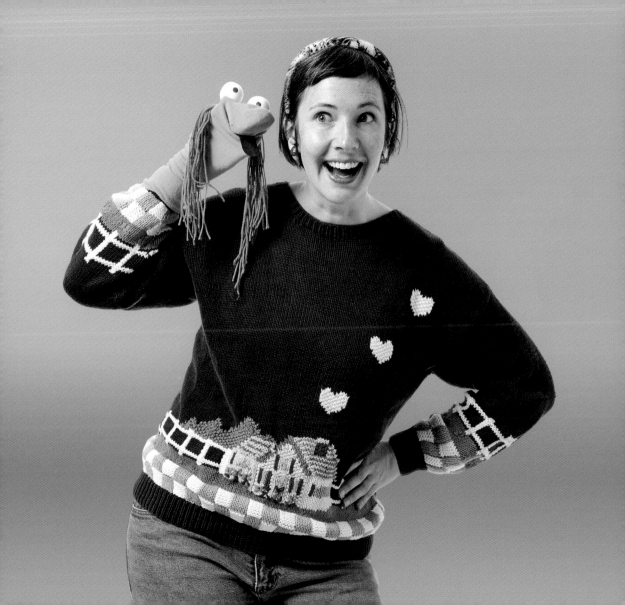

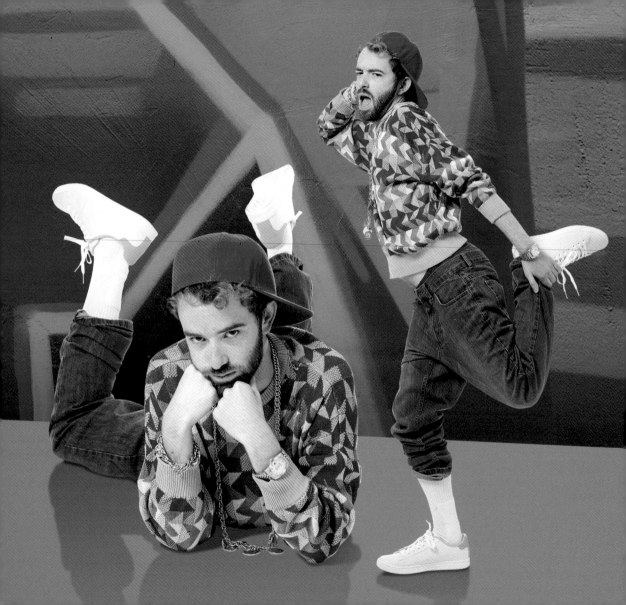

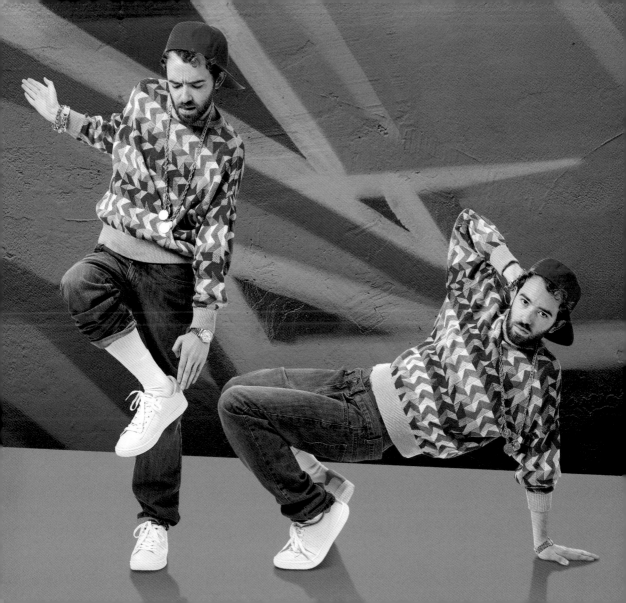

Hallå, vinter!

SAY HELLO TO SWEDISH FASHION THIS WINTER

Ja! Look at this rare find – The SVEÄTER. Back in the '80s it came flat-packed with 3x balls of yarn and 2x knitting needles. You had to make it yourself, but it was very reasonably priced.

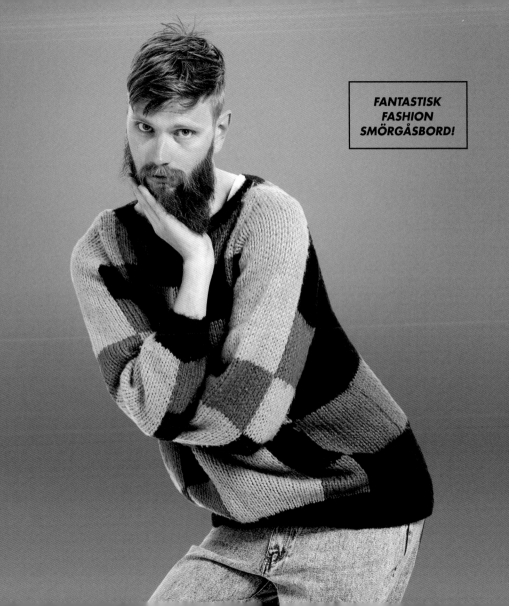

FANTASTISK
FASHION
SMÖRGÅSBORD!

Power lunch for one

WOMEN ARE WORKING – GET USED TO IT!

It can be tough for an independent business lady woman
to make it in a man's world. Fashion is your secret weapon!
Dazzle the CEO with a sweater featuring an explosion of
sequined flowers and red flair. Partnered with a sassy belt
and pencil skirt, this ensemble is sure to cut a formidable
silhouette in the boardroom.

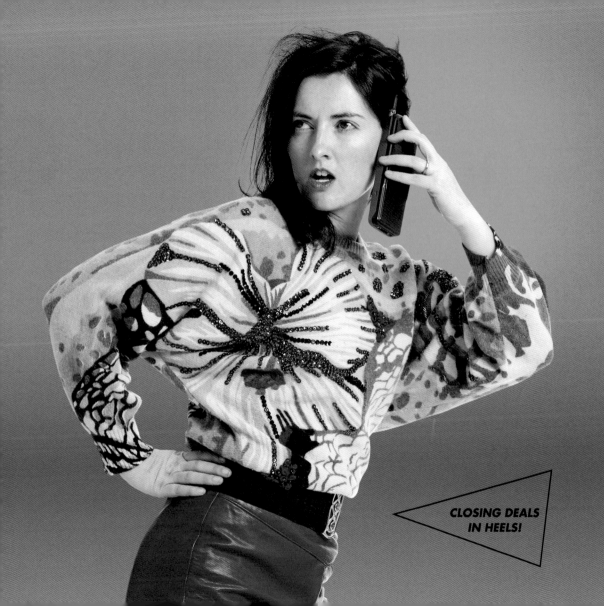

CLOSING DEALS
IN HEELS!

Tangled up in blue

HE'S NEVER GONNA DANCE AGAIN

We know you're hurting – breakups are hard. Drown your emotions in an ocean of cool, melancholy tones. This sweater could keep you warm. Not as warm as the sweet embrace of your former lover, but warm enough.

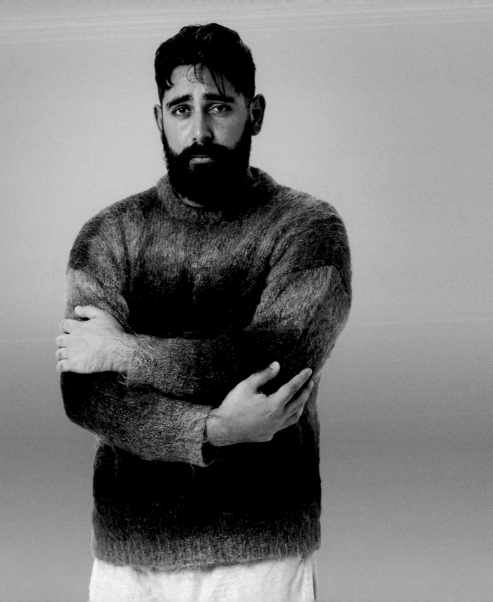

Fierce fleece

VERY VOGUE STYLES FRESH OFF THE RUNWAY

Paris, Milan, New York. Those are all places where fashion
happens. Take inspiration and create a cutting-edge look
that's as stylish as it is intimidating with a mohair cardigan
featuring swirls of chocolatey brown and gold froth.

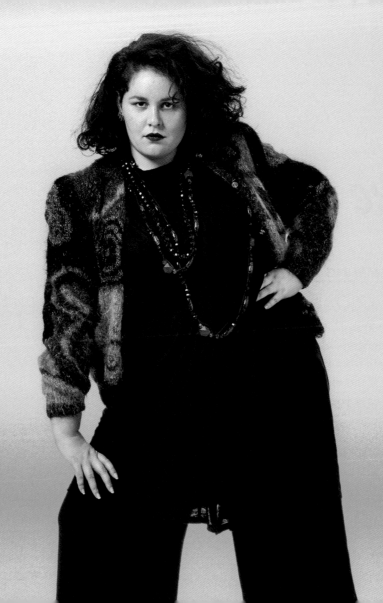

STRIKE
THE POSE

Take a hike!

SHE'S RAMBLING AGAIN

Show people you're the outdoorsy type by wearing a rugged expedition knit. This one is emblazoned with hiking boots and Native American–inspired zigzags. Secret pockets keep your trail mix safe from hungry bears. This garment also opens up into a tent if the emergency cord is pulled – a feature that could just save your life.

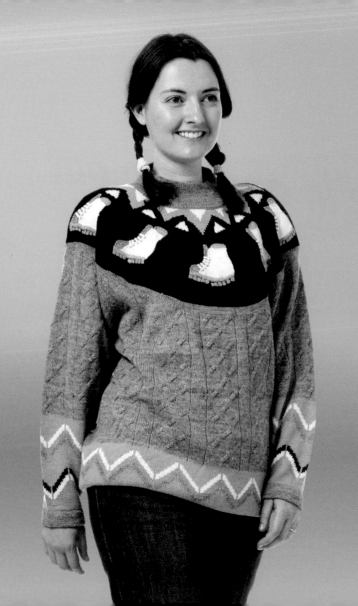

Tune in and drop out

ANALOG IS THE NEW DIGITAL

Finally, a sweater that celebrates both halves of your complex personality. While the bottom half of this garment cheerfully displays a test pattern with bright dancing shapes, the top half shows a more tortured scene of angry, frenzied static vibrating to post-punk.

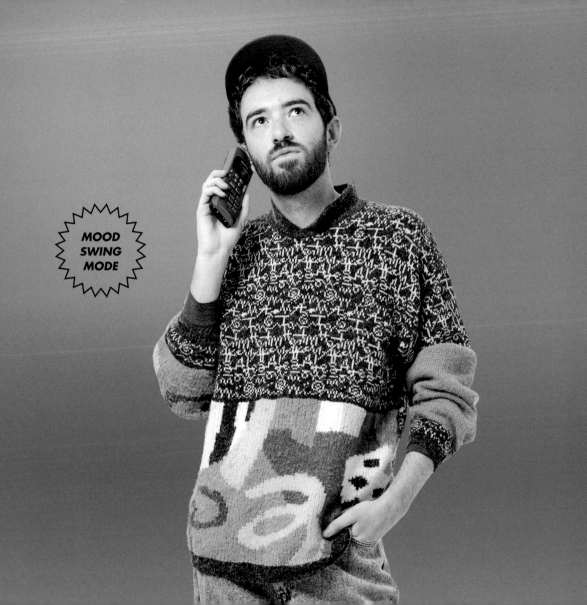

MOOD
SWING
MODE

Fun on the slopes

SNOW PLOW YOUR WAY TO STYLE

When visiting fashionable destinations, such as Aspen and St Moritz, it's important to look the part. A sophisticated penguin design like this one will assure you an avalanche of compliments from fellow skiers. Ideal for hitting the slopes after a dump of fresh powder or enjoying fondue and schnapps in the lodge.

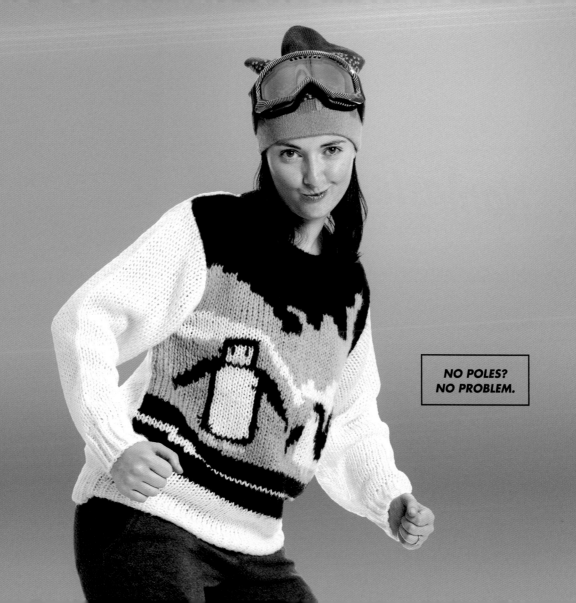

NO POLES?
NO PROBLEM.

Namaste!

HOT YOGA ACTIVEWEAR

There is more to yoga than stretching and holding in farts. It's also about detoxing. This crochet knit is made from 100% polyethylene terephthalate and designed to trap heat and promote extreme perspiration. It's like hot yoga for the price of regular yoga!*

*Single use only

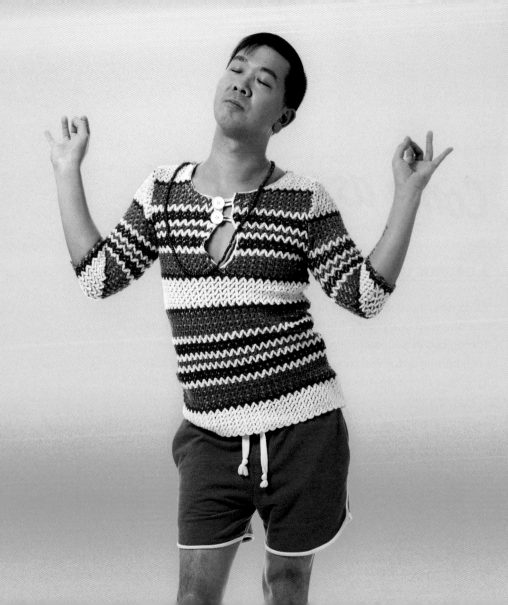

Come as you are

A GRUNGE LOOK THAT IS OH-SO HEROIN CHIC

What does teen spirit smell like? Our guess is a pungent mix of cheap bodyspray, hormones and fear. Feel stupid and contagious in a loose-fitting hooded sweater, like the one seen here in autumnal tones. Team with flannelette and glam sunglasses for a Seattle thrift store look that'll blow your mind.

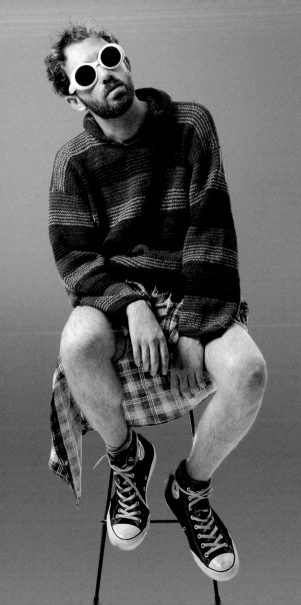

Coo-ee!

YOU GOIN' MY WAY, MATE?

You could hitchhike from Woolloomooloo to Wagga Wagga wearing this woolly work of art that showcases a swag of cultural clichés. Sections of the Australian flag, famous logos and native flora and fauna make up this one-of-a-kind piece. It's bloody bonza.

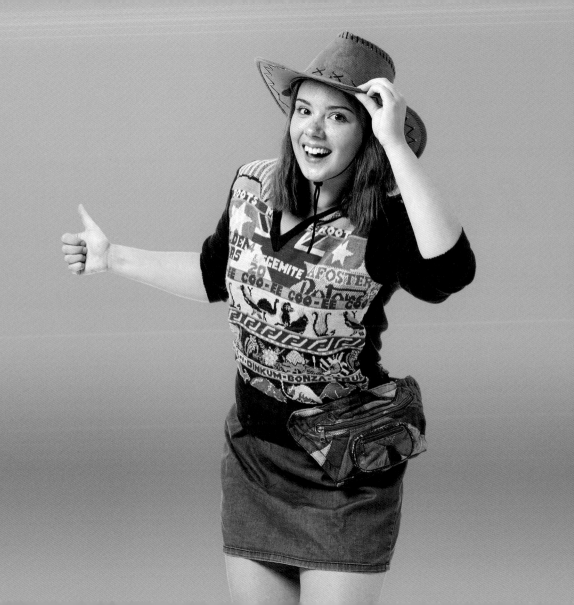

8-bit knits

FOR GAME BOYS AND GAME GIRLS

Get out your joystick and set the difficulty to hard! These Tetris-inspired knits are pixel perfect. Impress her with your sweet combo power moves and you're guaranteed to advance to the next level.

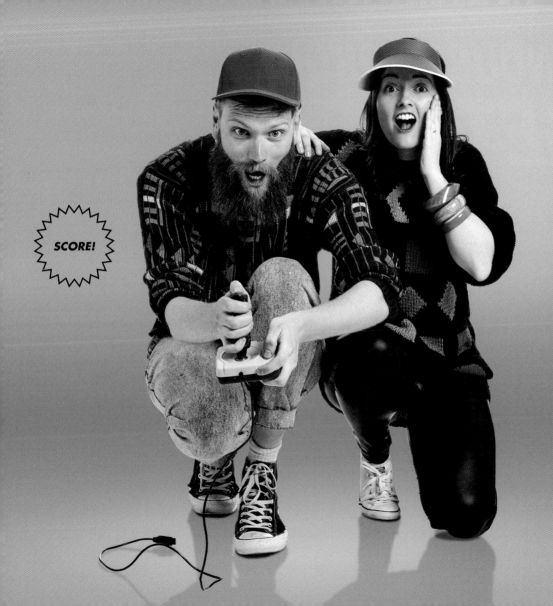

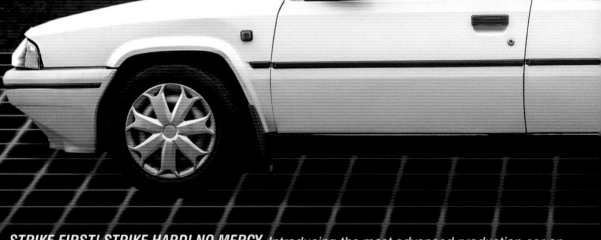

ENOUGH TORQUE.
GET IN.

STRIKE FIRST! STRIKE HARD! NO MERCY. *Introducing the most advanced production car on the planet. Two hundred horses of fuel-injected, turbo-charged thrust. Liquid crystal displays, on-board computer diagnostics, advanced electronics developed for jets. A cassette player and car phone. The future is here – but are you ready for tomorrow, today?*

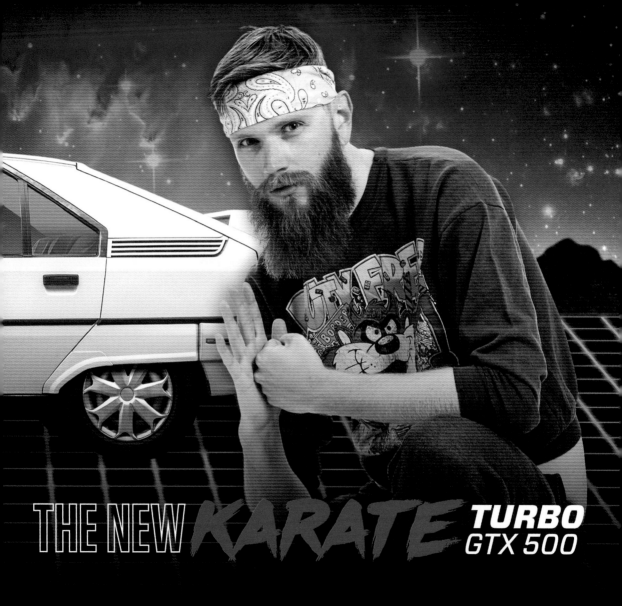

THE NEW **KARATE** **TURBO** *GTX 500*

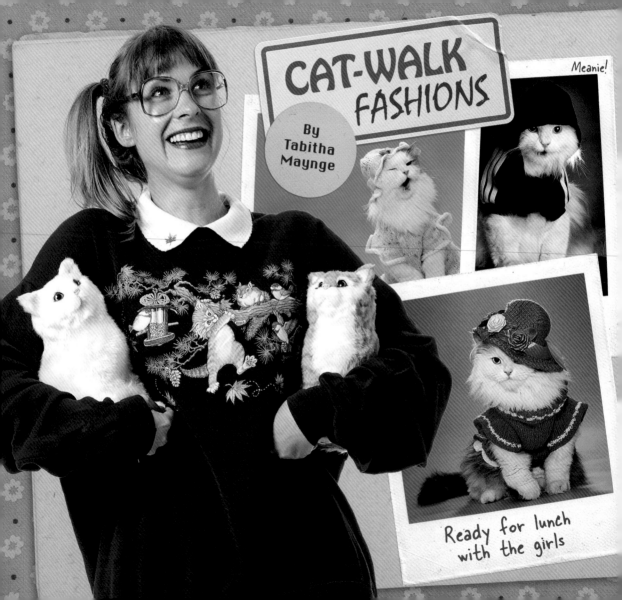

CAT-WALK FASHIONS

By Tabitha Maynge

Meanie!

Ready for lunch with the girls

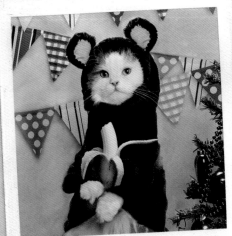

Cheeky Monkey

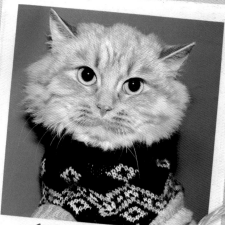

George, handsome
as always

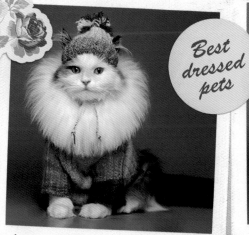

'Snow Lion' sweater
and hat combo

Best
dressed
pets

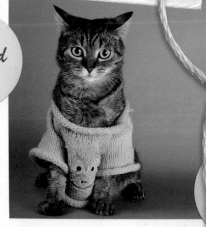

Cedric looking
'toadally' cool ☺

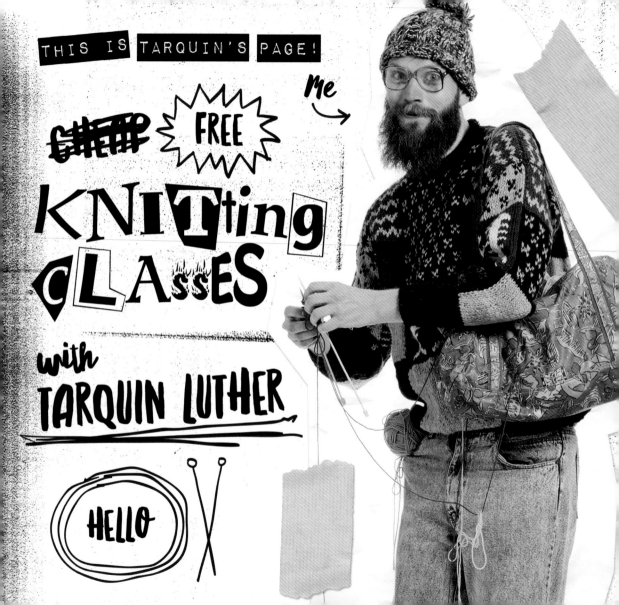

THIS IS TARQUIN'S PAGE!

Me →

~~CHEAP~~ FREE

KNITting CLAsseS

with TARQUIN LUTHER

HELLO

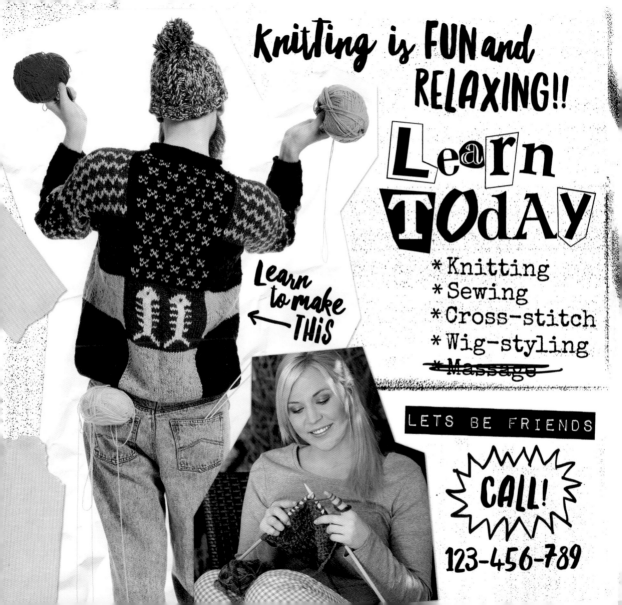

Knitting is FUN and RELAXING!!

Learn TOdAY

* Knitting
* Sewing
* Cross-stitch
* Wig-styling
* ~~Massage~~

Learn to make THIS ←

LETS BE FRIENDS

CALL!

123-456-789

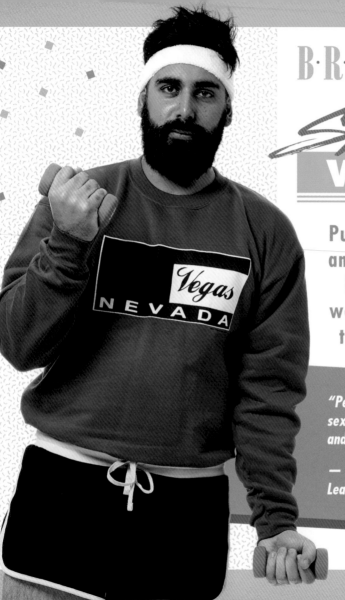

B·R·O·C·K STO·N·E

PRESENTS

Sweatshirt
WORKOUT

Put on your sweatshirt and get physical in this high impact aerobic workout with celebrity trainer, Brock Stone!

"Perspiration aids circulation, increases sexiness and helps rid the body of toxins and impure salts."

— BROCK STONE
Lean, mean, sweaty machine

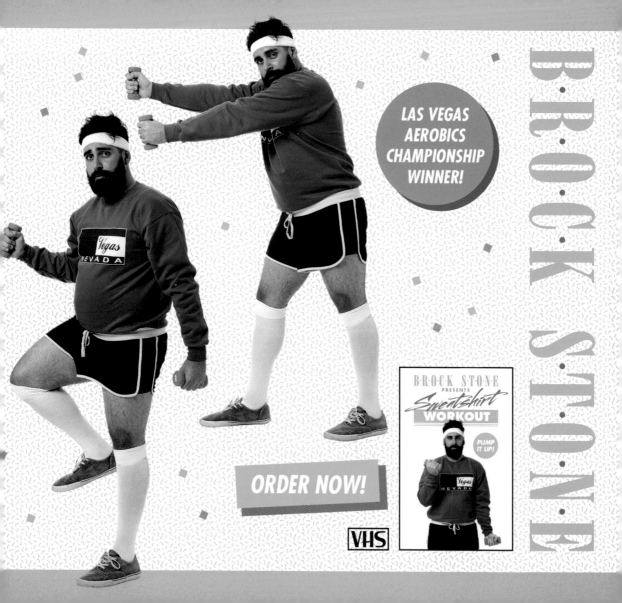

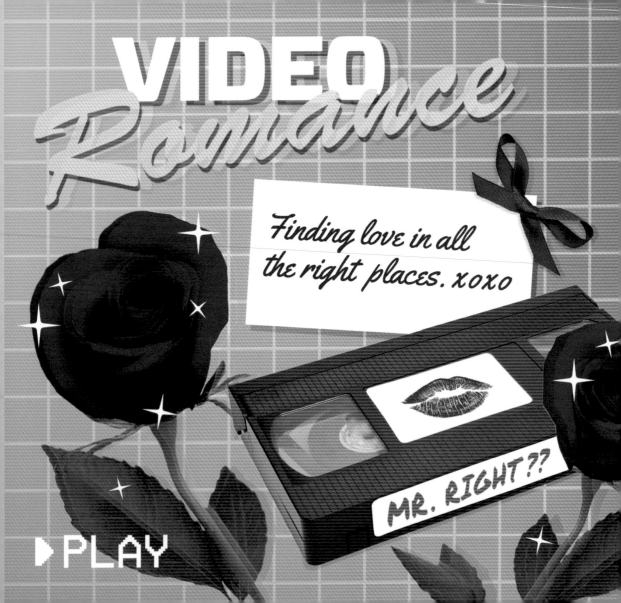

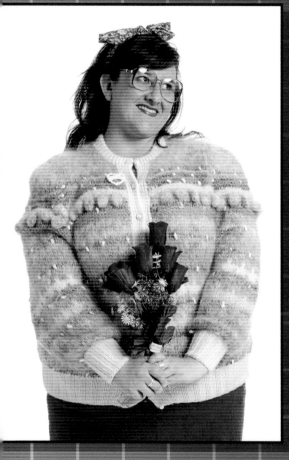

PROFILE

REF: #199202

ZODIAC SIGN: Virgo

HOBBIES: Magic (black), netball, microwave cookery, erotic pottery.

RELATIONSHIP: Never married.

CHILDREN: No, they are awful.

OCCUPATION: Kindergarten teacher.

WHAT'S YOUR JAM? Strawberry.

WHAT YOU DRINKIN'? Tepid water is fine.

PET PEEVE: When my pet ferret farts in bed. It's not funny, just annoying.

LOOKING FOR: A gentleman who is good with his hands and owns a car.

Fast-forward your love life.
Call 1800-VideoLove now!

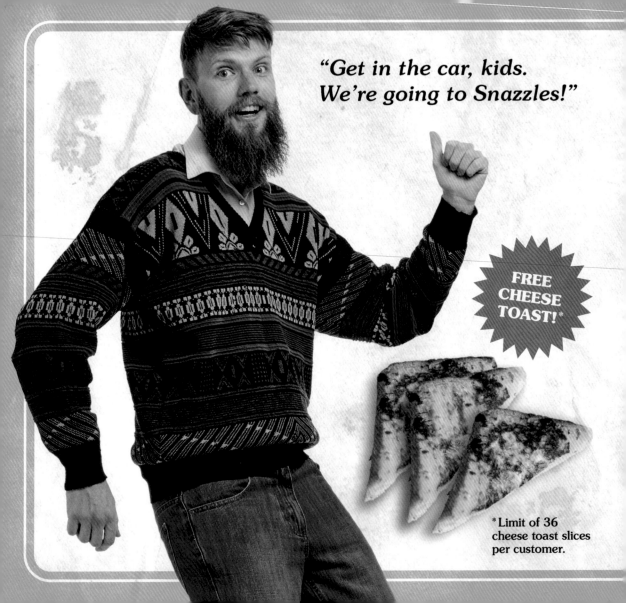

Quality. Choices. Great Value.

Here at Snazzles, we know you want choices. Buffet-style dining means you have the freedom to create your own culinary combinations just the way you want 'em. Creamy pasta bake and onion rings with a side of watermelon? No problem. We're here to support you in your questionable food decisions.

A BIT OF SNAZZLE IN EVERY BITE!

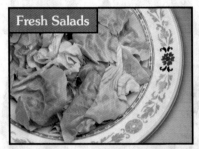
Fresh Salads

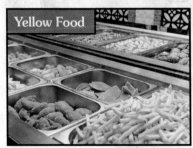
Yellow Food

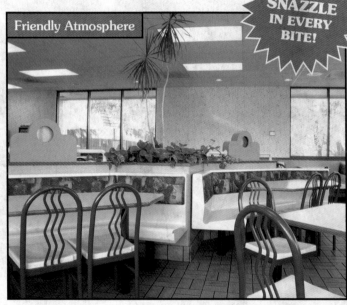
Friendly Atmosphere

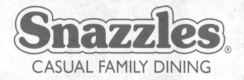
Snazzles®
CASUAL FAMILY DINING

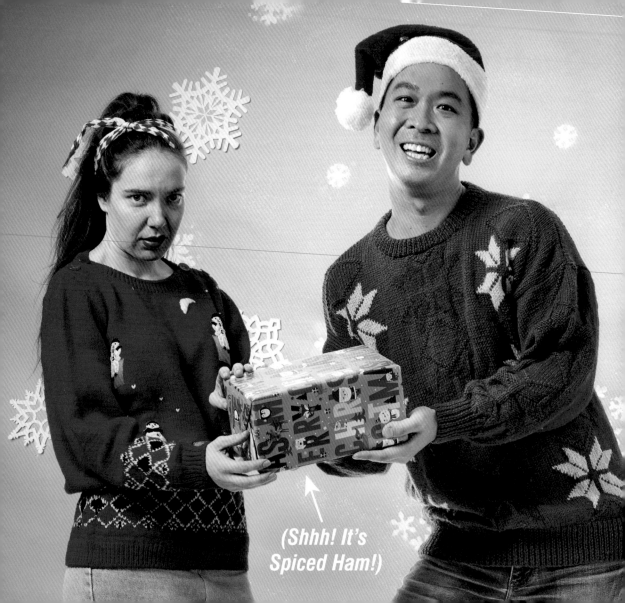

(Shhh! It's Spiced Ham!)

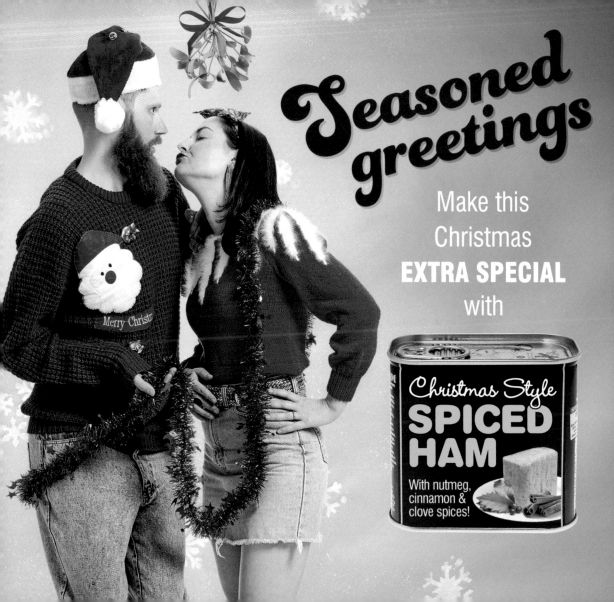

Def leopard

WELCOME TO THE JUNGLE

You're bound to score a backstage pass in a fierce animal sweater. Coupled with leather pants and chain belt, this wild knit would definitely bring out the animal in you and drive the band wild.

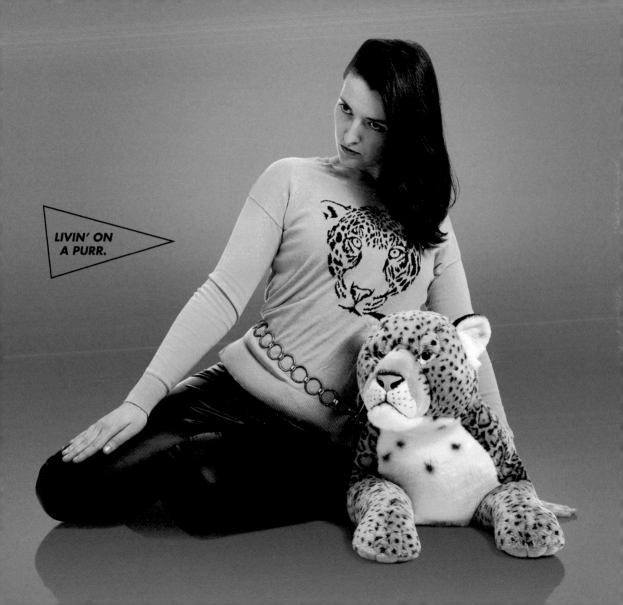

LIVIN' ON
A PURR.

Prince of springtime

FASHION TO GET YOU ALL A-FLUTTER

Emerge triumphant from your cocoon wearing a pretty sweater adorned with vibrant butterflies. This fine specimen is made from organic cotton and natural dyes derived from crushed beetle shells. Perfect for any collector.

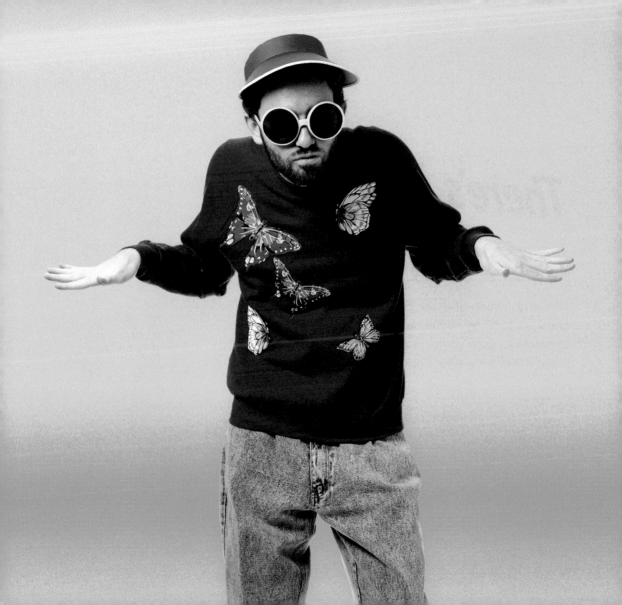

There's Nemo!

A LOOK THAT'S BOUND TO MAKE A SPLASH

Dive into a world of exotic tropical fish and vibrant coral.
Great for strolling on the beach or providing effective
camouflage when you're at the aquarium. Life really is better,
down where it's wetter, under the sea.

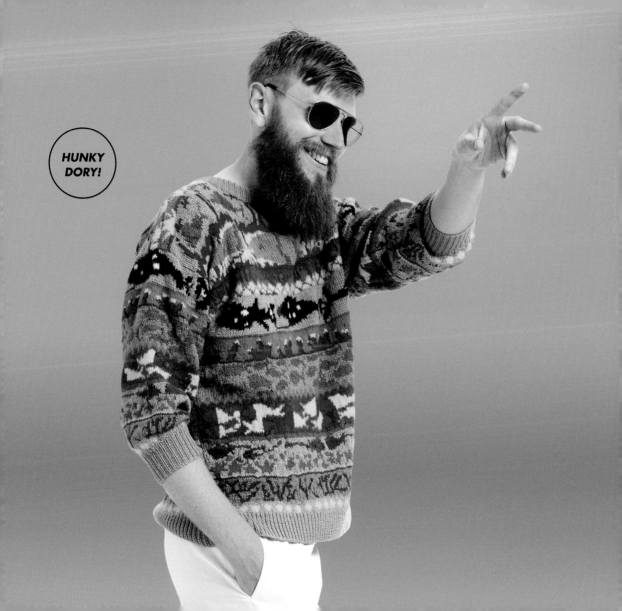

HUNKY
DORY!

Some fuuuuuuun!

SHOW YOUR TRUE COLOURS IN BLACK AND WHITE

A bat-wing sweater boasting fine floral detailing steals the spotlight in this ensemble. Contrast this delicate piece with a black lace skirt, edgy corset and fishnets, and you've got a look that's sure to be a hit time after time.

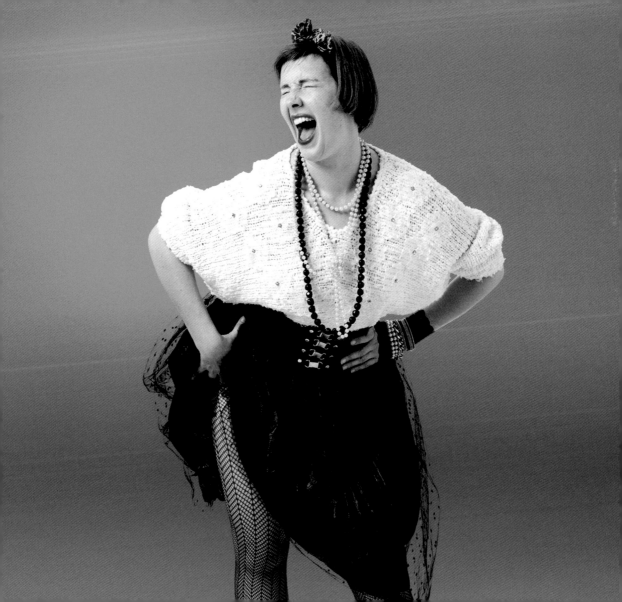

Feelin' yourself

YAK WOOL – THE ORIGINAL CASHMERE

Back in the '80s, everyone was talking about the soft but durable fur of Himalayan yaks – an exotic luxury so sensuous, you couldn't stop saying 'oohh' when it caressed your skin. Only the best yaks were selected, and then bathed in natural yoghurt to assure their fur was extra seductive and silky.

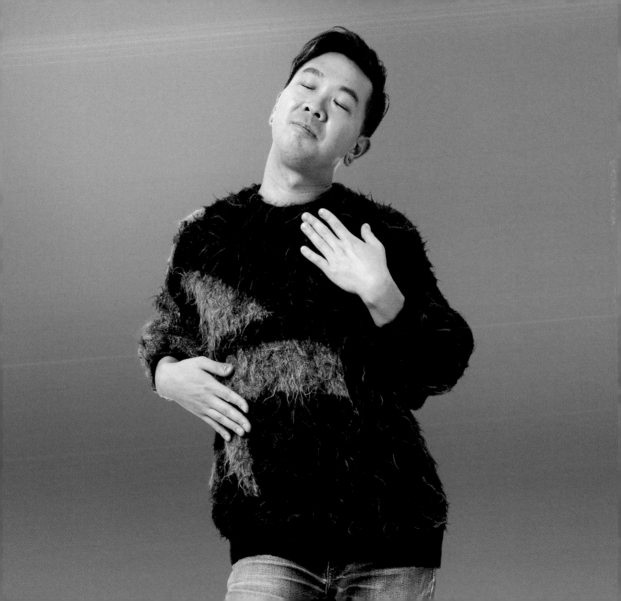

Ahoy matey!

A MARITIME STYLE THAT'S MAKING WAVES

Blistering barnacles! Navigate the treacherous waters of fashion in a nautical knit. This salty number celebrates the deadliest catch of all – the penguin. They're delicious with chips and mustard!

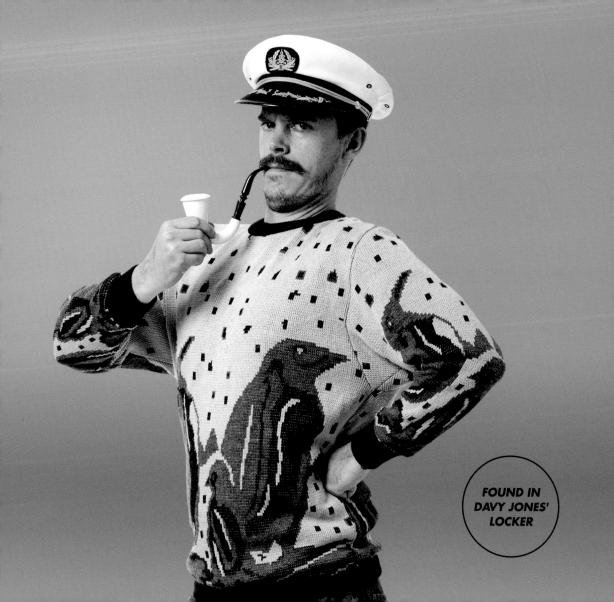

FOUND IN
DAVY JONES'
LOCKER

Feelin' fruity

PINEAPPLE? MORE LIKE FINEAPPLE!

Freshly hand-picked from a crop of sweet tops! This pineapple knit is crushing it. Shown here in a fruit salad of textures and prints, this variety of sweater is perfect for folks who pine for a summer look with a tropical punch.

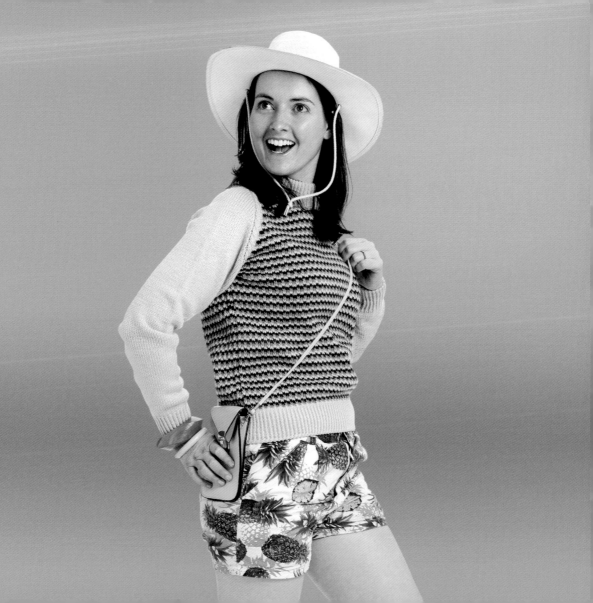

Fun in the sun

WE'RE SERIOUS ABOUT LEISURE

Turn heads on the beach this summer in a long-sleeve, textured cable knit. Made from waterproof AquaTech™ fabric*, this sweater doubles as a bathing suit so you can go from sand to surf without exposing your delicate, lily-white skin.

*AquaTech™ was discontinued in 1978.
 Do not expose to heat.

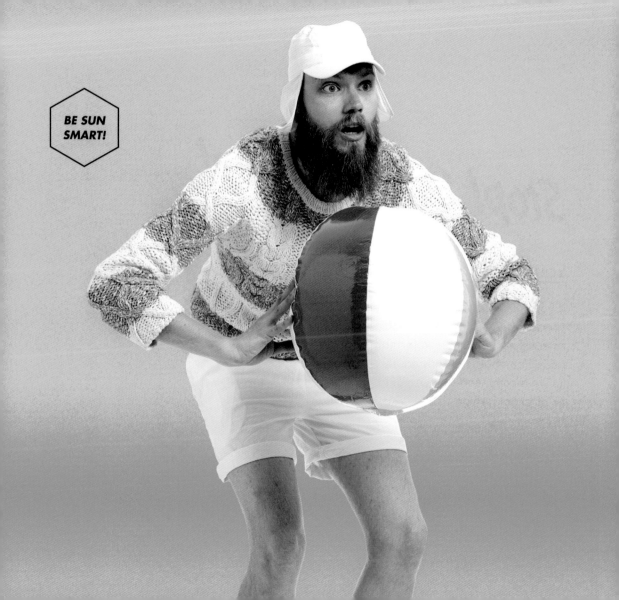

BE SUN
SMART!

Stop! Sweater time!

YOU *CAN* TOUCH THIS

If you are too legit to knit, then simply purchase a ready-made sweater from a vintage store. Go for a lightweight cotton, as it will allow you to comfortably bust out moves like a super dope homeboy. The girls are fly and the beats are kickin', so we recommend that you get hyped and break it down in an ol' skool fashion.

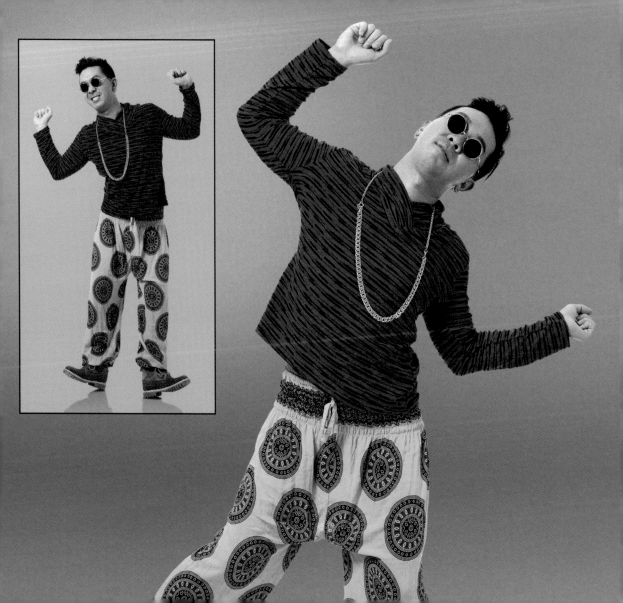

Let's go get 'em!

THERE'S NOTHING SWEET ABOUT THIS PINK LADY

This Friday night, skip the malt shop and go straight to make-out point in a bubblegum pink V-neck. Doll yourself up with shades and a sassy scarf to hide all manner of sins. There are worse things you could do!

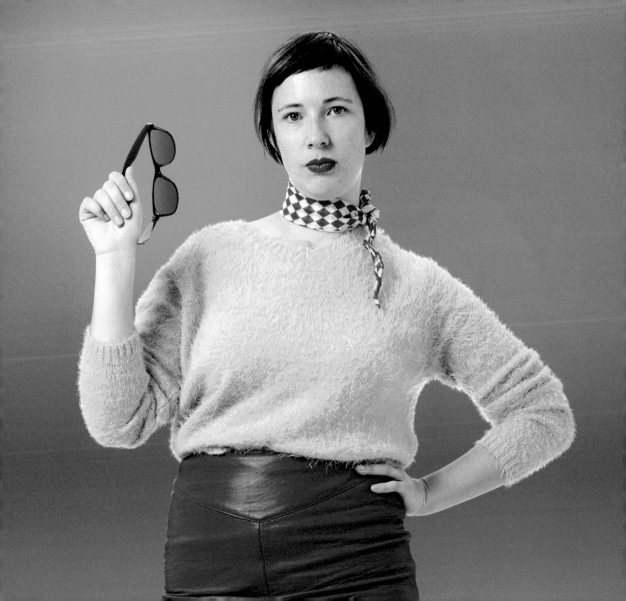

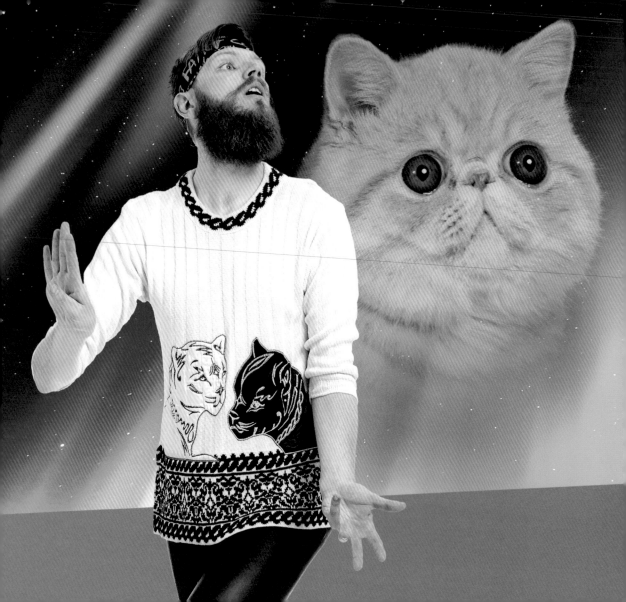

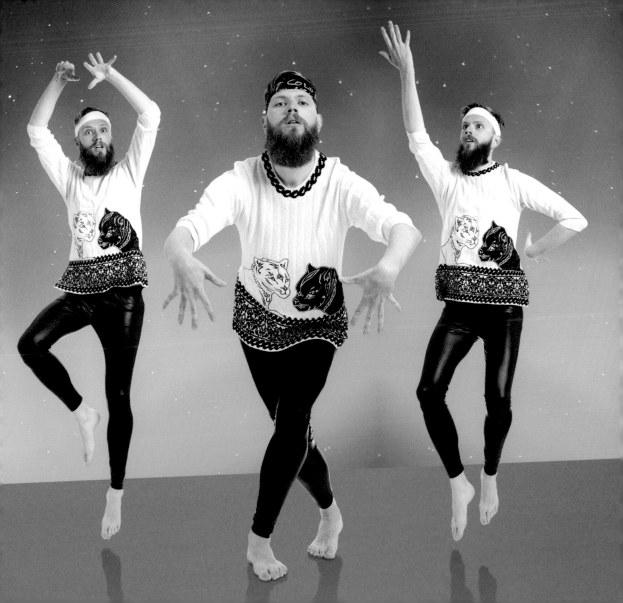

Armless fun

ADD A TOUCH OF CLASS WITH A FASHION CAPE

The sleeves on this sophisticated pure-wool cardigan are purely ornamental. You could throw it over your shoulders and meet the girls down at the local bistro for a cappuccino and sun-dried tomato focaccia. Maybe even a chardonnay – go on, why not!

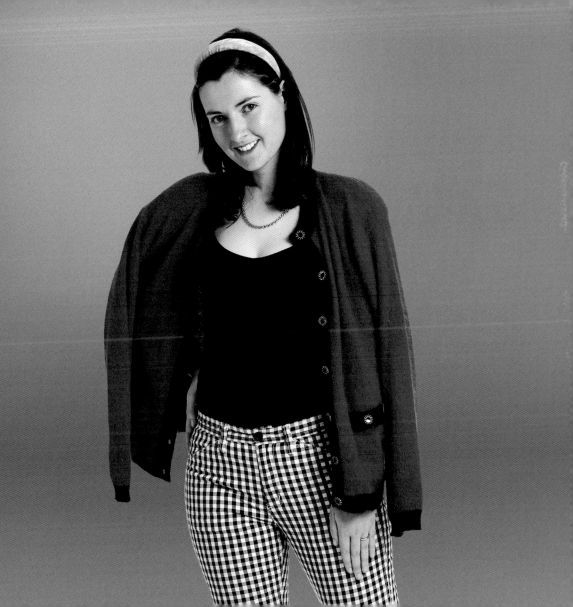

G'day, sport!

SKIPPY THE SNOW KANGAROO

Australians are proud of their native animals' achievements. It's a little-known fact that in the 1976 Winter Olympics, a kangaroo won gold in the downhill slalom. He was later disqualified for being a kangaroo, but his glory lives on through commemorative sweaters.

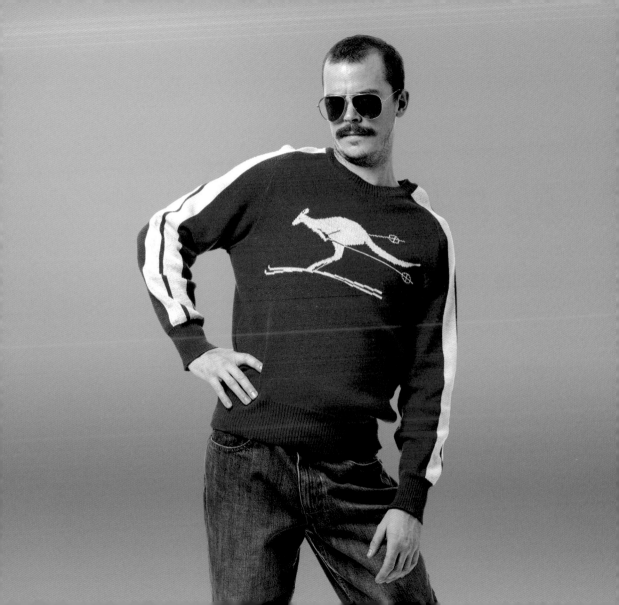

Big man on campus

MAKE THE CALL IN A HANDSOME CABLE-KNIT

It's not easy being Mr Popularity. There are football games to win, parties to attend and choices to make. Who'll score an invite to senior prom? Cindy? Sally? Mike? One thing's for sure, the lucky date will get a corsage and a mean case of beard burn.

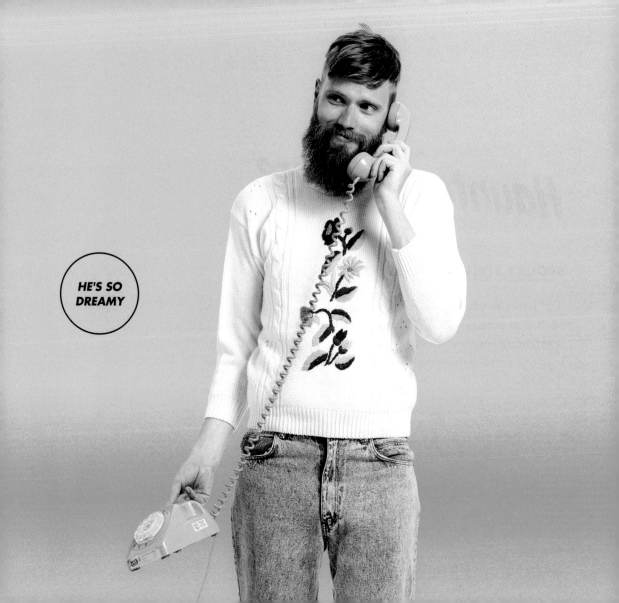

Haunted couture

SPOOKY STYLES FOR MEDDLING KIDS

Just because you're the brains of the group doesn't mean you can't look groovy too. A knitted cardigan in autumnal stripes and feature toggles will keep you looking stylish while solving mysteries and unmasking monsters. Don't forget your glasses! Jinkies!

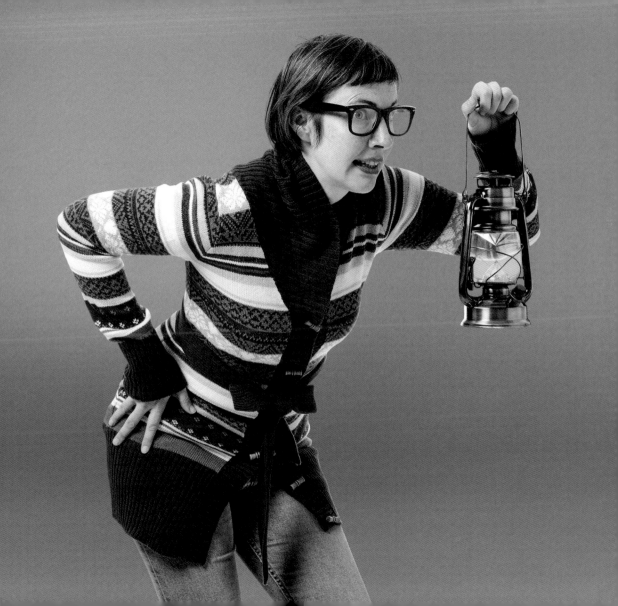

Singin' in the rain

WET WOOL WARNING

Singing in the rain seems like a fun idea but, in reality, water can damage your vintage knit and leave you smelling like a homeless chow chow. To remove the smell, we recommend gently hand-washing the garment in a nourishing shampoo with macadamia oil and jojoba extract. Because your sweater's worth it.

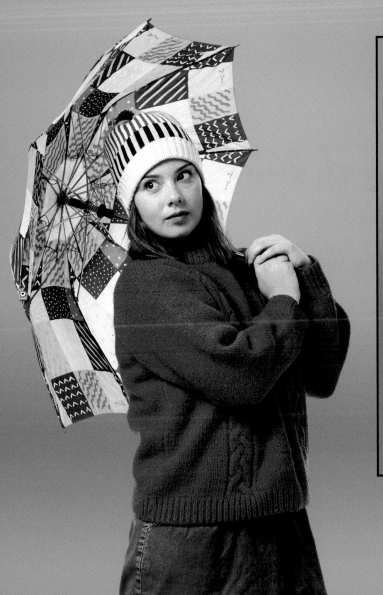
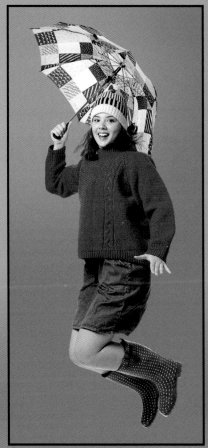

Springtime dreams

LOVE IS IN YOUR HEART, NOW AND FOREVER

You should enjoy the great feeling of this. You look OK.
Feel happy and refreshed as you walk through sakura with
your life partner. Now hear this! It's style.

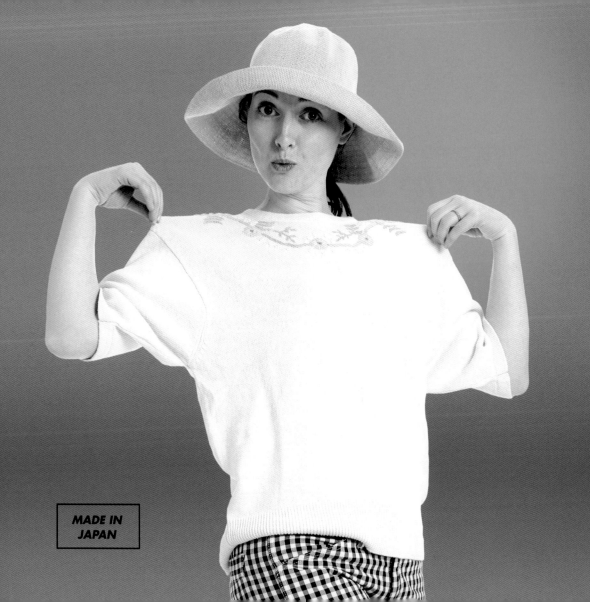

Yours to cherish

FEEL THE SOFTNESS IN YOUR HEART

Find comfort and tenderness in an easy-fit Fair Isle sweater with a classic abstract pattern. Soft and thick, it will keep you wonderfully warm on cold winter nights. Teamed here with a mustard pant and a beard that won't quit.

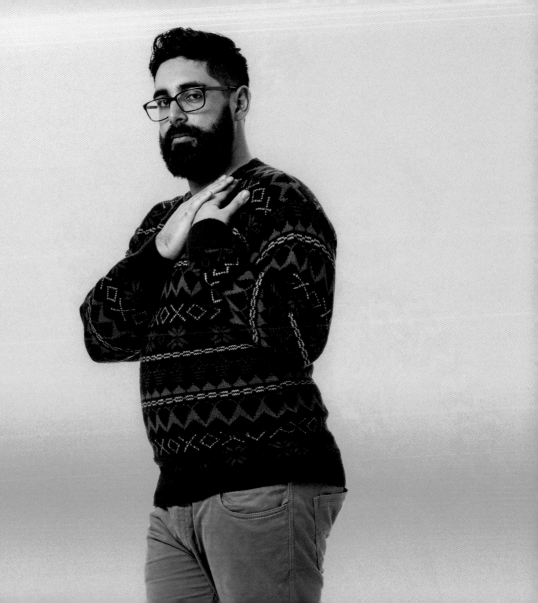

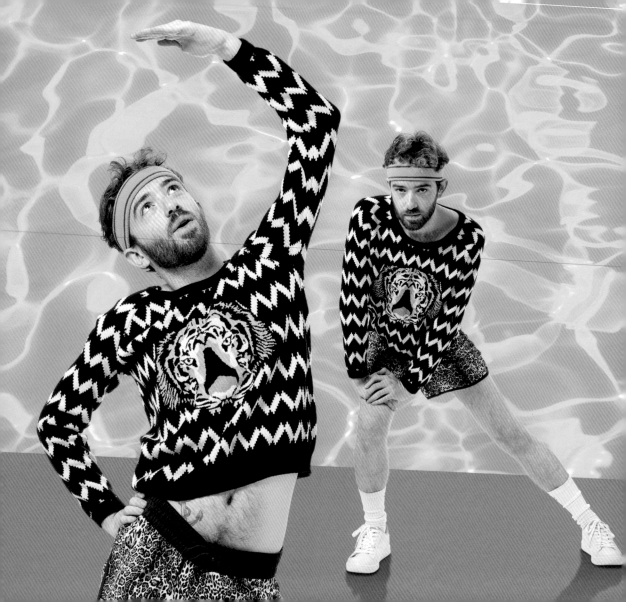

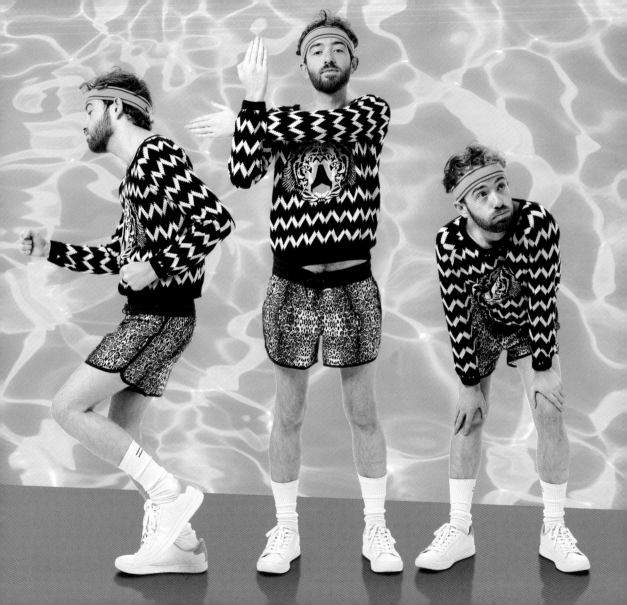

Look! Nature!

SCANDINAVIAN STYLE FOR THE GREAT OUTDOORS

Do you like cross-country skiing? Don't worry, nobody does.
But that shouldn't stop you from wearing an intrepid top
celebrating the national sport of Kalaallit Nunaat (Greenland).
This one features exhausted skiers, trees and flowers –
all embroidered by Nordic elves with tiny hands, so quality
is assured.

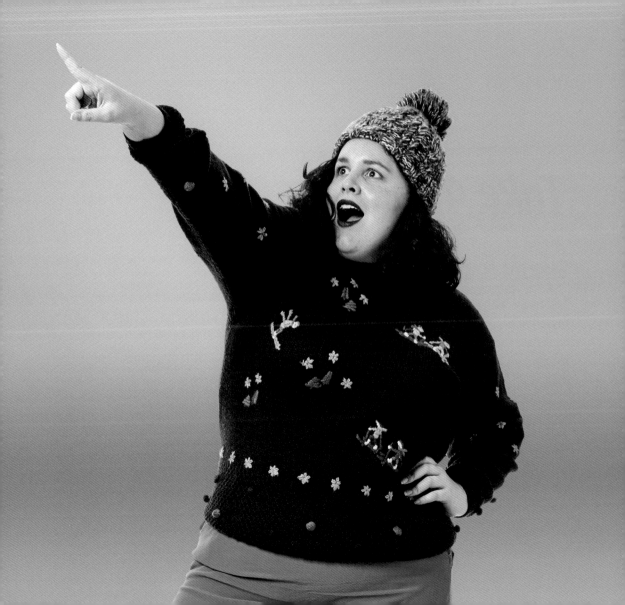

Take a trip

HEMP FASHIONS IMPORTED FROM GOA, INDIA

See music and hear rainbows in a psychedelic zip-up with
tasselled finishing. The perfect attire for enjoying a game of
hacky-sack or attending a psy-trance forest rave. No one is
stealing your thoughts, man. Chill.

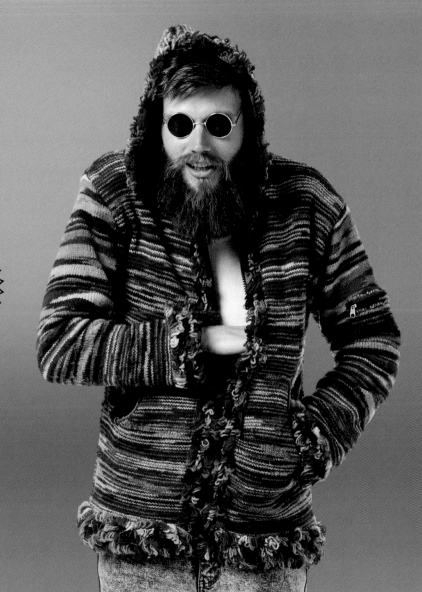

100%
HEMP

Sweaty memories

FEELIN' HOT HOT HOT IN THIS SWEATSHIRT

Here's a hot tip! This summer, take the 'Sweatshirt Challenge' and wear your vintage top for an entire week at the beach. Play volleyball, sunbake – maybe even meet the man of your dreams. The scent of pheromones, clams and seaweed will be permanently absorbed into the garment, leaving you with a treasured souvenir.

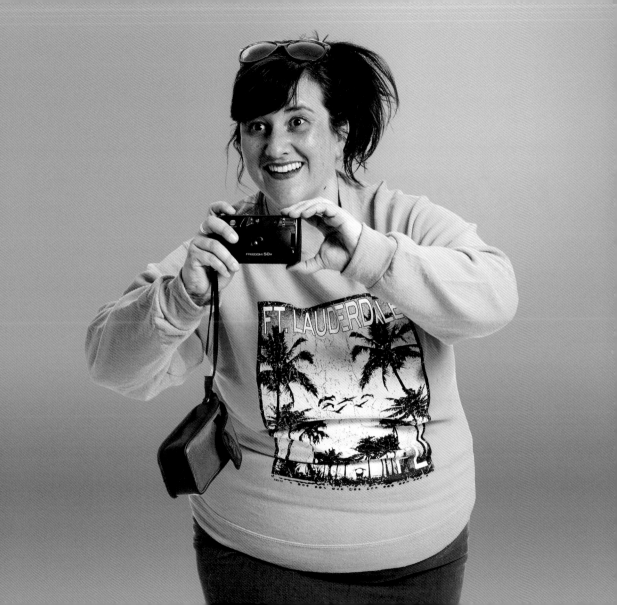

Pet portraits!

EVERY DOG HAS HIS DAY

Here's a fun craft idea – take a plain vintage sweater and then lovingly sew your best friend's face onto it. Rex, is that you? So lifelike! Cat, hamster and helper monkey portraits are also great. Ferret portraits are more challenging, as they refuse to pose for any length of time.

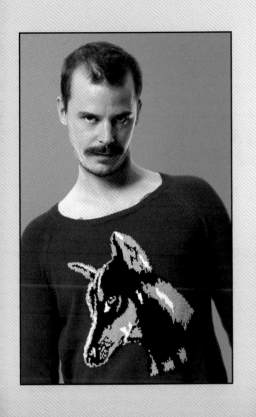
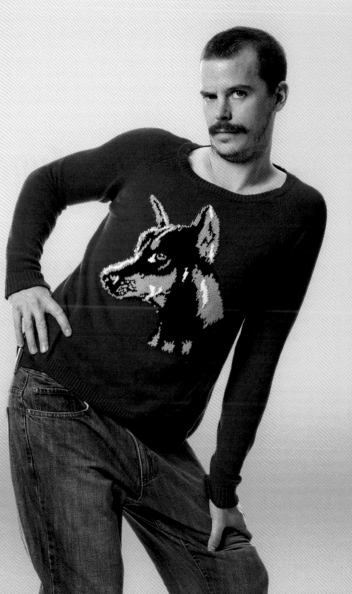

Too sassy to function

TALK TO THE HAND, I'M WEARING A SWEATER DRESS

Be unbearably sassy towards your friends and co-workers in a sweater dress. This indigo number features a cascade of hand-sewn sequins. According to science, sassiness levels can increase up to 40% when wearing a sweater dress. It's actually quite dangerous.

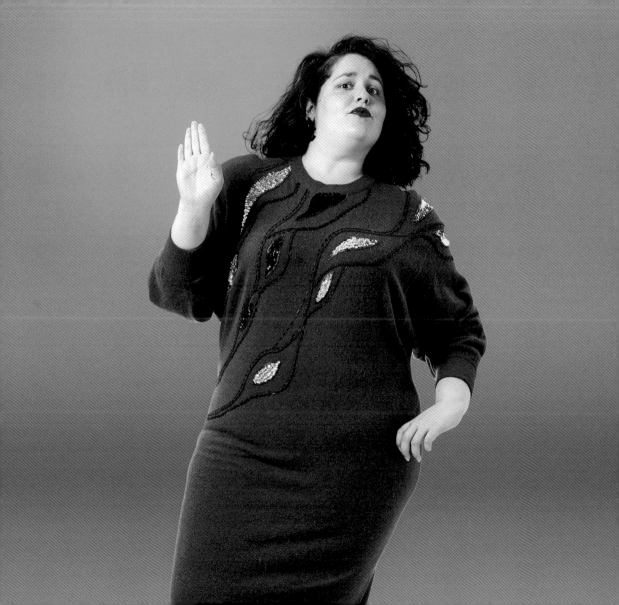

Painterly palette

NO HOMEWORK, JUST CHILL VIBES

This loose-fitting possum-fur sweater with overlapping swathes of dye would be perfect for a cool art teacher. You know, the kind of art teacher that takes everyone outside to trace leaves, or turns a blind eye to that 'decorative vase' in the school kiln.

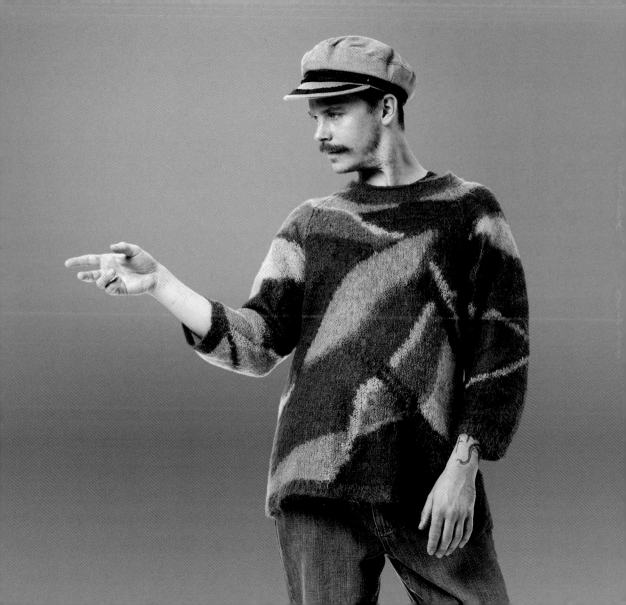

yacht club social

GET THE RICH-KID LOOK

Daddy's away in Monaco, so let's party on his boat! Jump on deck and impress your Ivy League pals in a cashmere crew neck in pastel tones. This preppy look is also perfect for rolling up to the polo club and poppin' crisp bottles on horseback.

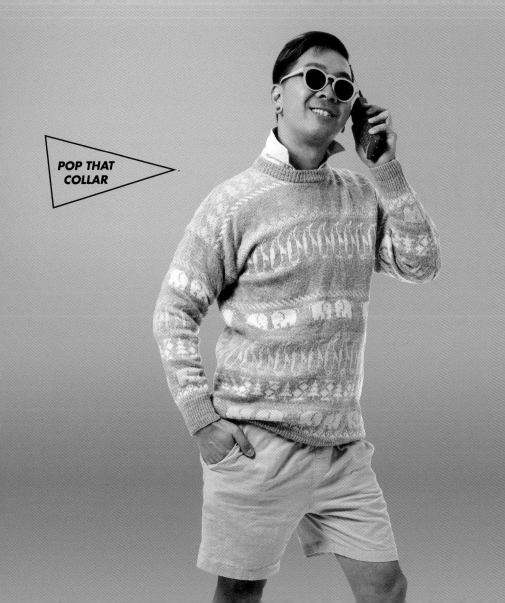

POP THAT
COLLAR

My little bronie

<u>SADDLE UP FOR FUN AND WHIMSY!</u>

Just because you watch cute pony cartoons in your parents' basement all day doesn't mean you have developmental problems. It just means you love friendship and magic! This purple ensemble is an homage to Princess Twilight Sparkle.

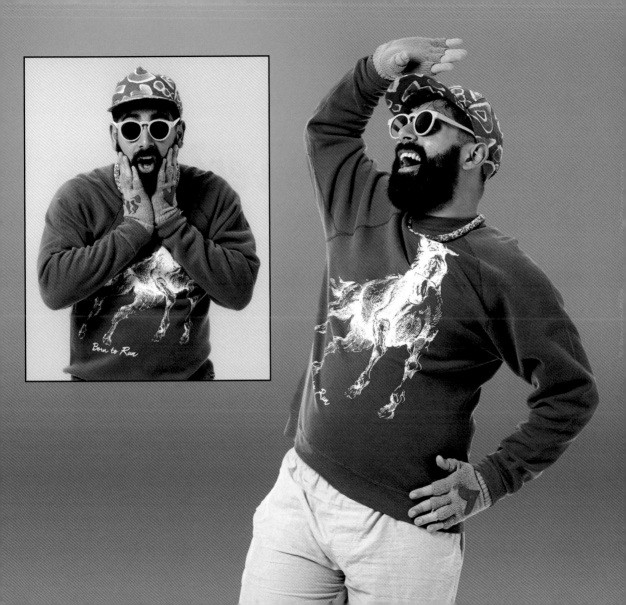

Wanna be my lover?

OWN THE NIGHT AND WEAR IT TIGHT

Look sexy and not creepy at all in a fitted dazzler made from the skins of animals. This wild design lets the ladies know that you possess the stealth of a leopard and the cunning of a snake. Gold chains and a Rolex you bought from a Russian man in your apartment complex complete the look.

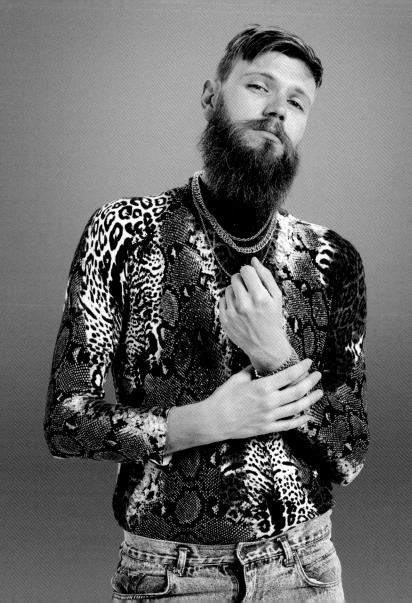

Garden state

KEEP SMILING! NEVER STOP SMILING!

What better way to break up the thankless tedium of being
a homemaker than spending a day in the garden. Dig up the
roses and then re-plant them, or chat to your reflection in the
bird bath. Team a floral sweater with pearls and a sunhat, and
you'll have a look to get the neighbours talking.

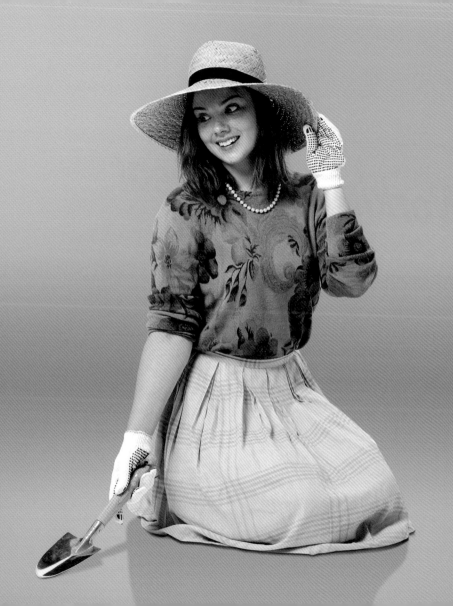

Workin' up a sweat

A WORKOUT LOOK THAT'S HOT ON TOP

If you want to get more personal with your personal trainer, you've got to sport a look that's athletic *and* sexy. Start with a full-length graphic sweatshirt promoting something tough, like duck hunting or the military, then add tiny shorts and a sweatband or visor. Oh yeah – witness the fitness!

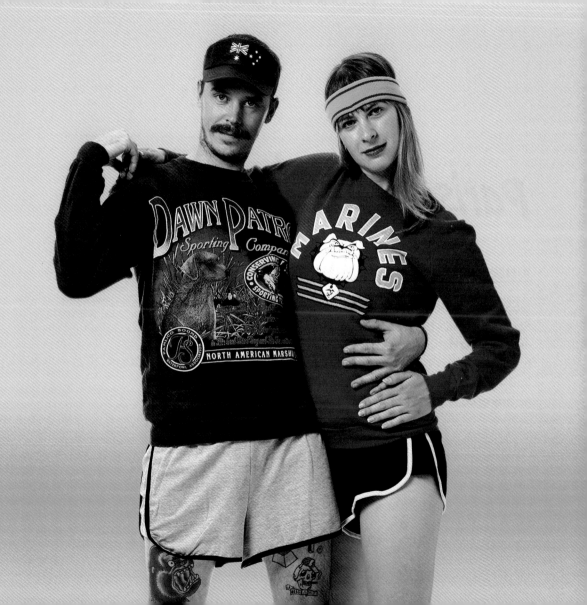

Paris du jour!

A NEW STYLE TO FALL IN LOUVRE WITH

Ooh là là! Say *bonjour* to fashion with an international flair. Paris is Europe's best-kept secret and is quickly becoming an unlikely destination for style and fashion. Pop a beret on your head and you've got the look. For a certain *je ne sais quoi*, add a *petit* handbag in which you can store three macarons – no more, no less. *Très bien!*

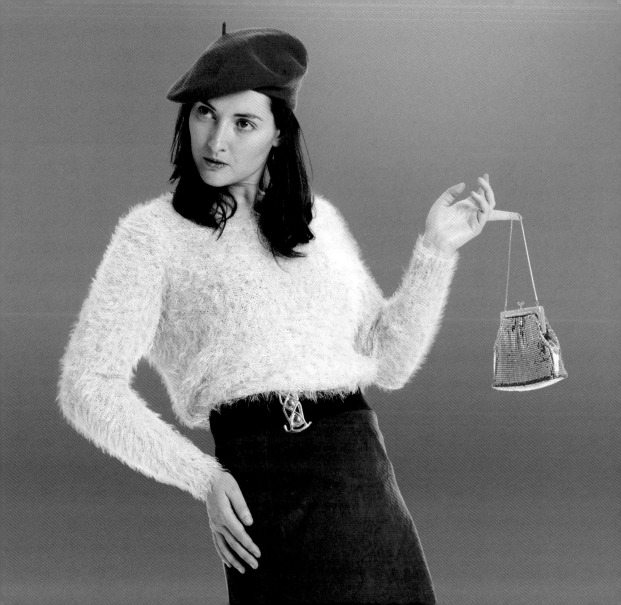

About the author

Simone Bennett is a Melbourne-based creative who formally trained as a graphic designer, but since graduating has branched out into a variety of creative fields including art direction, animation, illustration and now writing. Simone's passion for all things retro and kitsch has resulted in this book! When she's not pushing pixels, you'll find Simone thrift shopping for retro knick-knacks, dancing to '80s synth-pop or eating obscure snacks and then reviewing them on the internet. See @snackreview on Instagram to read more witty quips and snide asides.

THIS IS SIMONE, IN CASE YOU'RE WONDERING

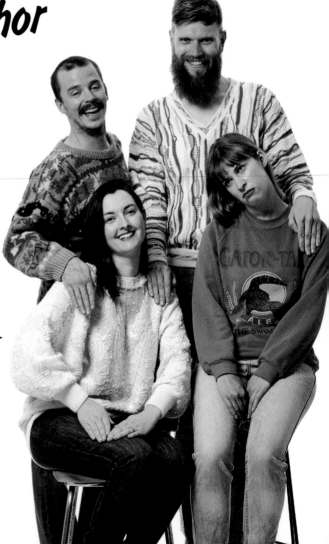

Acknowledgements

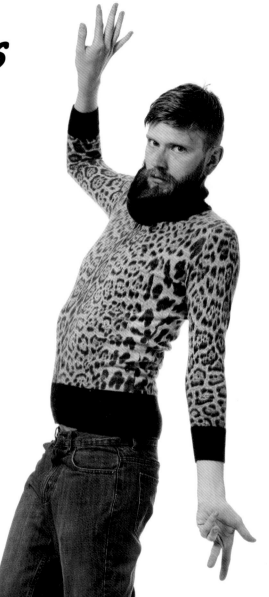

FABULOUS MODEL FRIENDS

Cassie McDonald, Andy Warren, AJ Singh Chahal, Sarah Strickland, Sarah MacAndrew, Ben Guiounet, Tagen Davies, Kate O'Donnell, Lauren Whybrow and Daniel Atkinson (my wonderful, supportive and sometimes weird husband, pictured right).

FASHION STYLING

Thank you to Kati Bottomley for making everyone look amazing and teaching me that a sweater can be tucked into jeans.

PHOTOGRAPHY

Thanks to Rich MacDonald and Ali Bailey for capturing the awkwardness perfectly in every shot.

CLOTHING HIRE

Shag, RetroStar Vintage and Rose Chong Costumiers. Thanks also to friends who lent me their beloved sweaters.

EXTRA AWESOMENESS

Tagen Davies and Lauren Whybrow – I owe you a beer.

PUBLISHER'S ACKNOWLEDGEMENTS

The publisher would like to acknowledge the following individuals and organisations:

Commissioning editor
Lauren Whybrow

Managing editor
Marg Bowman

Project editor
Lauren Whybrow
Kate J Armstrong

Editor
Kate O'Donnell

Photographers
Rich MacDonald
Ali Bailey

Stylist
Kati Bottomley

Pre-press
Megan Ellis
Splitting Image

Other photography credits
Stock images © Shutterstock/A_Lesik, Andris Tkacenko, Xiebiyun, GalapagosPhoto, kuban_girl, hannadarzy, P.D.T.N.C., absolutimages, Hong Vo, happy may, Picsfive, Scott David Patterson, Brooke Becker, AKaiser, Catherine Murray, Slavko Sereda, Ewais, photosync, Aleksandar Mijatovic, Petri jauhiainen; Dreamstime/ Konstantinos Moraitis

Published in 2016 by Hardie Grant Books, an imprint of Hardie Grant Publishing

Hardie Grant Books (Melbourne)
Building 1
658 Church Street
Richmond, Victoria 3121
hardiegrantbooks.com.au

Hardie Grant Books (London)
5th & 6th Floors
52-54 Southwark Street
London SE1 1UN
hardiegrantbooks.co.uk

Retro Jumpers
ISBN 9781741175165

Retro Sweaters
ISBN 9781741176223

10 9 8 7 6 5 4 3 2 1

A Cataloguing-in-Publication entry is available from the catalogue of the National Library of Australia at www.nla.gov.au

Colour reproduction by Splitting Image Colour Studio
Printed and bound in China by 1010 Printing International Ltd

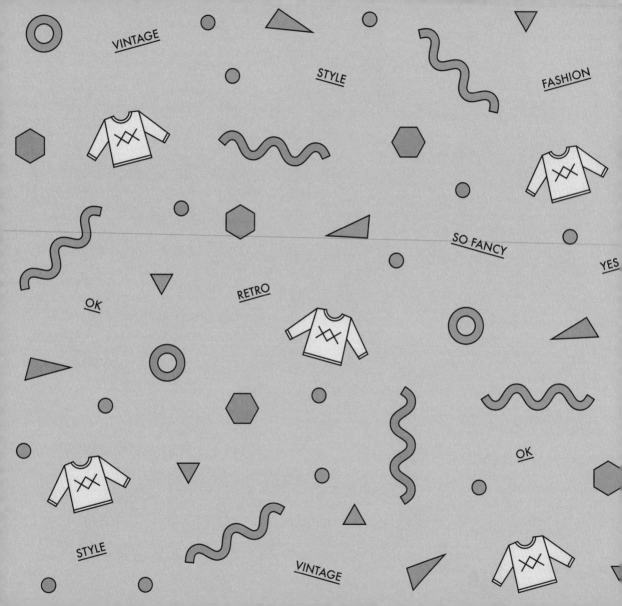